The Economics of Catholic Subsidiarity

Second Edition

D1648881

By: James A. DePrisco

www.jamesdeprisco.com

i

This book is dedicated to Shelby DePrisco. She died with a scapular on, and with the consolation of having saved a baby from abortion.

Preface to the Second Edition

The original edition of this book was released on Scribd, and mirrored on documents.mx. The last I checked it was still available. I created this second addition with some changes:

1. The "Realism" section in the first edition contained a prediction of economic collapse in 2013. That did not happen, averted by a level of money printing by the Fed that can only be called insane. I lost a bet on this prediction on a major Trad Catholic blog. So for this edition, I will not predict a date (I learned my lesson), but instead discuss the ramifications of our policy of economic statism.

2. I have cleaned up the first section and organized it better.

3. I have added a discussion of the "Calculation Problem", something I touched on in the first addition, but discuss more fully in this addition.

4. I have renamed the book "The Economics of Catholic Subsidiarity". In the first edition, I carefully used the term "economic libertarianism", and "Catholic Libertarian". I am not a Libertarian, however I chose these terms because people would have a general idea of the topic of this book.

5. I added a short discussion about the labor theory of value in the appendix.

Since revising the book, Donald Trump has been elected President. I have not updated the book to reflect this significant event. In short, President Trump will make some effective changes, specifically with regards to deregulation and trade, however I doubt he saves the country from a serious depression due to our $20 Trillion in debt.

Preface

In the Catholic world, we observe a wide variety of economic conditions. From Liechtenstein, Andorra, the Catholic cantons of Switzerland, and Monaco to the socialist fever swamps of Mexico, Bolivia, and Venezuela. All of these countries are (or were) Catholic. And yet they vary widely in their economic systems and living conditions. How can this be?

Or consider the United States, where in 2012 a majority of Catholics voted for leftist candidates, because they were leftists, and where a common feature of a "blue State" is the large proportion of Catholics residing there. Even more shocking was the support of Bishops for the Obamacare plan, the only obstacle being the funding of abortion. In fact the bishops didn't think this plan went far enough in its fascism and socialism!

One final example is the spectacle of the Notre Dame speech by Barrack Obama, where Catholics ignored the most pro-abortion beliefs ever in a President in order to honor him for his leftist policies. So much so that Catholic authorities had a pro-life 80 year old priest arrested and led off in handcuffs because: he was protesting abortion. Again, how can this be?

Ask a Catholic what the Sun King had to do with the French Revolution and the vast majority will only blink (he was a primary cause). Follow up with a hint, say, "John Law", and they still won't have a clue. Say, "usury with London bankers", and the response will be the same. And yet, if Catholics had learned the lessons from pre-revolutionary France, the USA might have been spared the Greater Depression.

The point has been made. There is vast ignorance in the modern Church, in the laity and the clergy, about economics. This is a sad situation primarily because the Church has the answers on how to properly structure an economic system. This book will present the Catholic economic system, which is the exact opposite of "Liberation Theology". In fact, it is best called "Catholic Subsidiarity".

The Economics of Catholic Subsidiarity

Check out www.jamesdeprisco.com for more discussions on Catholic economics.

INTRODUCTION

Start with this thought experiment: Imagine that you are driving down a super highway, driving at 70 miles per hour. However you are approaching a mountainous area, where the road becomes a windy, single lane highway with a speed limit of 45 mph, and no-passing for 15 miles. To your chagrin you come up to a car traveling 15 mph, right as you enter the no-passing zone. A stretch that should have taken 20 minutes to traverse will now take 1 hour.

Now capture the feeling you would have. It is a combination of anger and outrage. There is a reason why you feel this way, it is because there is an offense against justice, in this case distributive justice. The highway is available to everyone, and yet you are being deprived of your full driving rights because some idiot is only going 15 mph. Off on a tangent, the reason you feel anger over this injustice can not be reduced or explained any further. This feeling of anger over injustice is a proof that you have a soul.

Now, let us up the ante. Let us suppose that you find out that the idiot normally travels this stretch of highway at 50 mph, but seeing you in the mirror, he slowed down to 15 mph just to cause you grief. Let us up the ante even further. Let us suppose that the highway was supposed to be a 50-lane highway, but the legislature purposefully canceled those plans and changed it to a 1 lane road for the sole purpose of allowing the idiot to limit you.

It is very important for you to capture this "gut feel", because it is the same "gut feel" that should guide you in economics. On the one hand, if you have a 50 lane superhighway, then it doesn't matter if you have a control freak idiot on the road. There are 50 lanes **competing** for your driving, and if one lane is giving you poor service due to an idiot, you can try 49 other lanes. On the other hand you have the centralized one-lane road. Here you are forced to use this road, and any idiot can cause you grief. AND THERE IS NOTHING YOU CAN DO ABOUT IT. *What is more important is that the idiot knows there is nothing you can do about it.*

If you haven't already guessed, the 50 lane highway represents the 50 States of the USA. The one lane road is the Federal (Central) government, especially after the progressive assault in the early 20th century.

The model of the 50 lane highway is indeed the Catholic model for economics, and I shall present why that is, and in doing so, provide you with a moral sanction for free market economics.

1

WHAT THE CHURCH TEACHES

THE ENCYCLICALS

To begin a discussion on economics, as Catholics it is best to start with what the Church actually teaches on the subject. Not some expert or other, but the Church itself. And there is no better source than the Papal Encyclicals. Below is a group of papal decrees extracted from the relevant encyclicals.

On Subsidiarity

1. "It is a fundamental principle of social philosophy, **fixed and unchangeable**, that one should not withdraw from individuals and commit to the community what they can accomplish by their own enterprise and industry. So, too, **it is an injustice** and at the same time **a grave evil and a disturbance of right order**, to transfer to the larger and higher collectivity functions which can be performed and provided for by lesser and subordinate bodies. – (Pope Pius XI, *Quadragesimo Anno*, 79)"

2. "it becomes a duty to give to the indigent out of what remains over. "Of that which remaineth, give alms."(14) It is a duty, **not of justice** (save in extreme cases), but of Christian charity - **a duty not enforced by human law**. -- (Pope Leo XIII, *Rerum Novarum* 22)"

On Private Property

3. "The first and **most fundamental principle**, therefore, if one would undertake to alleviate the condition of the masses, must be **the inviolability of private property**. This being established, we proceed to show where the remedy sought for must be found." --RN

4. " 47. In order to place definite limits on the controversies that

have arisen over ownership and its inherent duties there must be first laid down as foundation a principle established by Leo XIII: The right of property is distinct from its use.[30] That justice called commutative commands sacred respect for the division of possessions and forbids invasion of others' rights through the exceeding of the limits of one's own property; but the duty of owners to use their property only in a right way does not come under this type of justice, but under other virtues, obligations of which **"cannot be enforced by legal action."**[31] Therefore, they are **in error** who assert that ownership and its right use are limited by the same boundaries; and **it is much farther still from the truth** to hold that a right to property is destroyed or lost by reason of abuse or non-use." -- QA

5. "That We, in keeping with Our fatherly solicitude, may answer their petitions, We make this pronouncement: Whether considered as a doctrine, or an historical fact, or a movement, Socialism, if it remains truly Socialism, even after it has yielded to truth and justice on the points which we have mentioned, cannot be reconciled with the teachings of the Catholic Church because its concept of society itself is utterly foreign to Christian truth. ....
Religious socialism, Christian socialism, are contradictory terms; no one can be at the same time a good Catholic and a true socialist." – QA

6. "Let them, however, never allow this to escape their memory: that whilst it is proper and desirable to assert and secure the rights of the many, yet this is not to be done by a violation of duty; and that these are very important duties; **not to touch what belongs to another**; to allow every one to be **free in the management of his own affairs**; not to hinder any one **to dispose of his services when he please and where he please**. – (Pope Leo XIII, *LONGINQUA)"*

7. "38. Here, however, it is expedient to bring under special notice certain matters of moment. First of all, there is the duty of safeguarding private property by legal enactment and protection. Most of all it is essential, where the

passion of greed is so strong, to keep the populace within the line of duty; for, if all may justly strive to better their condition, neither justice nor the common good allows any individual to seize upon that which belongs to another, or, **under the futile and shallow pretext of equality**, to lay violent hands on other people's possessions." – *Rerum Novarum*

On the Form of Government

8. "Nor can it be believed that Our words are inspired by sentiments of aversion to the new form of government or other purely political changes which recently have transpired in Spain. **Universally known** is the fact that the Catholic Church **is never bound to one form of government more than to another**, provided the Divine rights of God and of Christian consciences are safe. She does not find any difficulty in adapting herself to various civil institutions, be they monarchic or republican, aristocratic or democratic. – (Pope Pius XI, *DILECTISSIMA NOBIS)*"

9. "Again, it is not of itself wrong to prefer a democratic form of government, if only the Catholic doctrine be maintained as to the origin and exercise of power. Of the various forms of government, the Church does not reject any that are fitted to procure the welfare of the subject; she wishes only - and this nature itself requires - that they should be constituted without involving wrong to any one, and especially without violating the rights of the Church. – (Pope Leo XIII, *LIBERTAS)*"

On Labor Unions and Guilds

10. "Furthermore, if Catholics are to be permitted to join the trade unions, these associations **must avoid everything that is not in accord, either in principle or practice, with the teachings and commandments of the Church or the proper ecclesiastical authorities**. Similarly, everything is to be avoided in their

literature or public utterances or actions which in the above view would incur censure.

The Bishops, therefore, should consider it their sacred duty to observe carefully the conduct of all these associations and to watch diligently that the Catholic members do not suffer any harm as a result of their participation. The Catholic members themselves, however, should never permit the unions, whether for the sake of material interests of their members or the union cause as such, **to proclaim or support teachings or to engage in activities which would conflict in any way with the directives proclaimed by the supreme teaching authority of the Church**, especially those mentioned above. Therefore, as often as problems arise concerning matters of justice or charity, the Bishops should take the greatest care to see that the faithful **do not overlook Catholic moral teaching and do not depart from it even a finger's breadth.** -- (Pope Pius X *Singulari Quadam*)"

11. "Let them, however, never allow this to escape their memory: that whilst it is proper and desirable to assert and secure the rights of the many, yet this is not to be done by a violation of duty; and that these are very important duties; not to touch what belongs to another; to allow every one to be **free in the management of his own affairs**; not to hinder any one **to dispose of his services when he please and where he please**." -- LONGINQUA

Basic Concepts

The subject of Economics is based on a few key concepts derived from the Catholic Church and also Metaphysics. The concepts include the following: that man is fallen and ruled by Original Sin, that man is not omniscient, the principle of Subsidiarity, the Cardinal Virtue of Justice, including commutative and distributive justice, and finally the Cardinal Virtue of Prudence. In order to understand economics, a prudent understanding of reality (I repeat myself) must be grasped. Therefore I will write in detail upon these subjects.

Prudence: The chief Cardinal Virtue presented by the Church, given the pride of place as the First cardinal virtue is prudence. Unfortunately in modern parlance, the classical meaning of the word "prudence" has been all but lost, instead now understood to be synonymous with "pragmatic". This is a grave error. For example, we can easily describe a "pragmatic" man as someone who would deny Christ in order to save himself from being martyred; however a truly "prudent" man would embrace martyrdom. Prudence means simply this: **to align ourselves with reality**, which reality includes that God exists, that there is a heaven and a hell, and that Jesus is our Savior and Lord. The Truth is beautiful.

The Fallen Nature of Man: "What truly is the point of departure of the enemies of religion for the sewing of the great serious errors by which the faith of so many is shaken? They begin by denying that man has fallen by sin and been cast down from his former position. Hence they regard as mere fables original sin and the evils that were its consequence. Humanity vitiated in its source vitiated in its turn the whole race of man; and thus was evil introduced amongst men and the necessity for a Redeemer involved. All this rejected, it is easy to understand that no place is left for Christ, for the Church, for grace or for anything that is above and beyond human nature; in one word the whole edifice of faith is shaken from top to bottom." – (Pius X, *Ad Diem Illium Laetissimum*, Feb 2, 1904)

Man is a fallen race. This simple fact is today denied almost everywhere, but it remains true. Modern man, atheists, agnostics, and yes many (most?) Catholics deny this basic premise, though the latter is mostly seen as an implied denial. An important book written on the underlying philosophical principals behind the modern collapse, *Atlas Shrugged* by Ayn Rand, goes a step further and has as its underlying premise that the *belief* in Original Sin is the root of our evils. This is a huge irony as the majority of the book describes a society of fallen men. Furthermore, converted communist David Horowitz in his book *Radical Son* states that the denial of Original Sin is the fatal flaw of leftists, as he relates that the traumatic murder of his friend was the catalyst that eventually led him to accept that man was fallen, and that an earthly utopia was impossible. After that realization, he could no longer continue as a communist.

The concept of Original Sin and its effects were clearly presented by St. Augustine in his *City of God*. In this book he explains that the Earth is the City of Man, the City of the Devil. It is at war with God and His Church. God's elect and those temporarily in the Church form the City of God. The inhabitants of the City of God are mere sojourners on Earth, constantly at war with the City of the Devil. As long as we are on Earth, a utopia is impossible for any of us. What St. Augustine wrote about over 1500 years ago was experienced by Mr. Horowitz in our present day.

The effects of Original Sin are identified by the Church: 1. Our intellects are clouded. Clearly **Man is not omniscient**. 2. Our passions are enflamed. 3. Our wills are weakened, e.g. we will tend to choose the easy immediate course over the proper course involving sacrifice and delayed reward.

A prudent economic system MUST accept the fallen nature of

man, or it will utterly fail. In fact, an economic system that does not take into consideration our fallen state is by definition imprudent.

<u>Justice:</u> The Church lists Justice as another Cardinal Virtue. Justice is simply this: receiving what we are owed. This virtue can be abstracted to a higher level: that we have the ability to be "owed". However, we can go no further. There is no explanation of how someone can be in our debt, or how we can be in debt to another, though both are Truths. There is a reason why we can not explain justice any further. We can be owed only because of our <u>spiritual</u> side. In fact, a strong proof that God exists is the natural *feeling* of Injustice that we experience when we are denied what is our due, or observe others being denied their due. It wells up from our <u>soul</u>. An atheist is incapable of explaining what we know to exist, because Justice emanates from God. In fact, He is described as "All Just".

The Church has further divided Justice into three types: Legal, which concerns our duty to obey the (moral) laws of society, commutative, which is what we owe to others in the PRIVATE sphere, and distributive, which is what society owes us out of PUBLIC goods and services. A prudent economic system must be especially concerned with the latter two. For in commutative justice lies the basis for trade. That I should receive what I am owed for my work, and that a "just" trade will only occur if **we exchange value for value**.

The next form of justice, Distributive Justice, is unfortunately named for modern man and is today almost completely misunderstood. We are oftentimes given the example of the poor man juxtaposed with the rich man, being told that this is not in accord with a fair distribution of goods, and thus offends distributive justice. In a word distributive justice has been twisted to mean communism. The error occurs because the term "goods" is not further limited to PUBLIC goods. If the rich man worked for his wealth, and a poor man spent his time in drunkenness, then this wealth disparity is in accord with commutative justice. Distributive justice does not apply in this situation.

In fact the concept of Distributive Justice paradoxically means the exact opposite of what the Peace and "Justice" crowd takes it to mean. An example illustrates this point: the property tax. Suppose in a town the (public) government concerns itself only with providing roads and street lights. To pay for these PUBLIC services it imposes a property tax. It can be easily seen that in this case the property tax is an offense against distributive justice as the owner of higher valued property pays more, even though he "uses" the street lights and roads the same as someone without any property. The rich man does not receive his fair "share" of street lights and roads. For this simple example the only tax that would be in accord with Distributive Justice would be the poll tax, which is a fixed fee paid by everyone, or perhaps everyone that drove a car. The response of the Peace and "Justice" crowd to this would be predictable.

Private Property: I will only re-quote what I previously recorded in the Encyclical section. No further comment is needed: "The first and **most fundamental principle**, therefore, if one would undertake to alleviate the condition of the masses, must be **the inviolability of private property**. This being established, we proceed to show where the remedy sought for must be found." and

"In order to place definite limits on the controversies that have arisen over ownership and its inherent duties there must be first laid down as foundation a principle established by Leo XIII: The right of property is distinct from its use.[30] That justice called commutative commands sacred respect for the division of possessions and forbids invasion of others' rights through the exceeding of the limits of one's own property; but the duty of owners to use their property only in a right way does not come under this type of justice, but under other virtues, obligations of which "**cannot be enforced by legal action**."[31] Therefore, they are **in error** who assert that ownership and its right use are limited by the same boundaries; and **it is much farther still from the truth** to hold that a right to property is destroyed or lost by reason of abuse or non-use."

"38. Here, however, it is expedient to bring under special notice certain matters of moment. First of all, there is the duty of safeguarding private property by legal enactment and protection. Most of all it is essential, where the passion of greed is so strong, to keep the populace within the line of duty; for, if all may justly strive to better their condition, neither justice nor the common good allows any individual to seize upon that which belongs to another, or, **under the futile and shallow pretext of equality**, to lay violent hands on other people's possessions." *Rerum Novarum*

Subsidiarity: Taken into consideration the previous concepts, the Church presents to us an economic system, which is termed Subsidiarity. Subsidiarity was best described by Pope Piux XI in *Quadragesimo Anno*, previously cited, which bears repeating: "It is a fundamental principle of social philosophy, fixed and unchangeable, that **one should not withdraw from individuals and commit to the community** what they can accomplish by their own enterprise and industry. So, too, **it is an injustice** and at the same time a grave evil and a disturbance of right order, **to transfer to the larger and higher collectivity functions which can be performed and provided for by lesser and subordinate bodies**."

The basis of subsidiarity is pushing governance to the local, community level as much as possible. This system is a natural conclusion to the underlying Catholic premises. By placing governance at a local level, subsidiarity respects the fallen nature of man, for example his clouded intellect. For while a local government will never be 100% correct, it will tend to be more

11

"correct", much more, then a distant central government. Man is not omniscient, so it is impossible for a distant form of government to know the proper direction a society needs. A local government will clearly have more knowledge of local affairs, and tend towards the right outcome.

Furthermore, by decentralizing governance to a local level, competition will be introduced. Competition, as I will show over and over again, acts as a check against the fallen nature of man, as a person is free to move to a more just community if his local government behaves in an evil manner. Competition is a vital element in a prudent economic system. In the case of governments competition is oftentimes called "voting with your feet", which was clearly demonstrated by the (ex) residents of Detroit. The push by the Progressives in the early 20th century to install a central bankers' guild (the Federal Reserve), a national income tax, and to trample States' rights is a clear witness to the power of "voting with your feet", which power our enemies realized had to be eliminated.

In addition to the Progressive attack, the leftist element in the Church has tried to eliminate the doctrine of subsidiarity by inserting a Hegelian dialectic into the Catholic definition as can be seen by this new definition circulating throughout Catholic literature: "A community of a higher order should not interfere in the internal life of a community of a lower order, depriving the latter of its functions, (thesis) but rather should support it in case of need and help to **coordinate** its activity with the activities of the rest of society (antithesis), always with a view to the common good (synthesis)." I believe that this definition was introduced by Cardinal Schoenborn, known for his recent homosexual blessings in his cathedral, and his resistance to the Pope installing conservative Bishop Wagner in Austria, who was forced to resign. But I digress.

The new definition introduces an ambiguous term (a common

strategy of the Modernists as seen by the writings of Vatican II): **coordinate**. Now coordinate could mean that the central government provides limited support and benchmarking, or it could mean that the central government takes over a dictatorial function. The above definition is ambiguous. You can guess which way the Modernists interpret it.

Another attack against Subsidiarity has come about by introducing a novel "virtue" called "Solidarity", which is used to limit subsidiarity, nay even to completely neuter it. This "virtue" appears to have been created by Father Heinrich Pesch, SJ, as related by this quote from an article by Thomas Storck in *New Oxford Review*: "and it is from Pesch that John Paul II has taken many of the ideas of his own social encyclicals, including the idea of man as the subject of work, of man's dominion over the world as founded on his exercise of work, **and even the key term "solidarism" (solidarity).**" Solidarity therefore is a novelty, dating from around 1900 A.D., and not a Traditional Catholic virtue. It can't be, as there has to be a plethora of caveats to go along with it, e.g. being in solidarity with your government in support of abortion is NOT virtuous. In many modern writings this novel "virtue" is used to neutralize the teachings on subsidiarity, as "solidarity" leads naturally to a powerful central government.

As far as Pesch, the following quote, without comment, will give you an indication as to whether he can be taken seriously: "In order that a general consensus [on prices] may establish itself in the most concrete and **objective** terms, it is advisable to set up organizations within which producers, merchants, and buyers can express their **views**." Unfortunately it appears Pope Pius XI relied on Pesch for certain troubling sections of *Quadragesimo Anno* and *Divini Redemptoris*, which I will discuss later.

One last thing we have to thank Pesch for is the creation of the term "social justice", again a novelty. Now consider, if we use the traditional meaning of "justice", in a society of strict social justice people who do not work starve. "Social justice" usually means "social mercy", but the leftists don't want to point out that your alms should be voluntary, as the Church requires.

These attacks against Subsidiarity, however, can not abolish the Truth: that man is fallen. And giving power to fallen men is a very dangerous enterprise, hence the importance of Subsidiarity, pushing power down to diffuse local governments. As Catholic Lord Acton noted: "power corrupts, and absolute power corrupts absolutely".

FURTHER DERIVED CONCEPTS

The Iron Law of Economics: I describe the Iron Law as originating from metaphysics because it is merely a statement of necessity. The Iron Law states the following: "In order to consume, you must first produce". This applies to a just economic system. However, the absolute form of the Law is this: "In order to consume, SOMEONE must first produce". In order to diagnose a problem in an economic system, we do well to start with the Iron Law. An example will illustrate this. In our current Greater Depression we are told that there is a lack of demand, and thus we need "stimulus". This is very imprecise, and in fact erroneous. As a horse owner I will gladly pay someone $1 a day to haul manure. I will also gladly pay someone $1 to install a new roof for my house every year. In fact it is not much of an exaggeration to say that demand is infinite. The obvious response to the above example is that it is not feasible for someone to install a new roof on my house for a dollar if he wishes to cover his costs, let alone provide for himself. That is correct, and we now have turned our attention to PRODUCTION, which allows us to begin isolating the problem. The reason why someone is not employed putting a new roof on my house every year is NOT due to a lack of demand, but due to PRODUCTION costs.

As an aside, we can analyze the concept of "stimulus" further. We can imagine a program to pay people to dig a hole, and then fill it back up. This will provide "stimulus" to the economy through

14

wages. However in reality this is wasteful CONSUMPTION, and in fact the recipient of the "stimulus" would be much better off if the government just handed him the money, as he would still have available to him what is termed the most valuable resource: Time.

The Iron Law of Economics is useful because it directs our attention to the most vital Question when analyzing economic problems: "Why can't people PRODUCE?".

Determination of Allocation: This is the "problem" that economics attempts to solve: how to best allocate scarce resources, including property, raw materials, finished goods, labor, and services. An example will demonstrate the problem. Consider Frank who is a miller. He owns a section of land for wheat production and a mill, producing 150 sacks of flour a day. Ben is a sole proprietor who collects wild wheat berries and hand grinds them to flour. He produces 2 sacks of flour per day. Ben has no trouble selling his flour due to the purported "natural" benefits of his flour, but is limited due to a lack of capital. Frank realizes that if he hires Ben, he can increase production to 200 sacks per day. Ben will be paid in sacks of flour. As head of the planning Soviet for flour production, you must determine how much Ben should be paid. What is the "fair" or "correct" wage that Frank should pay Ben?

Now consider the possibilities: The living wage doctrine can be satisfied by paying Ben 2 sacks per day, as he is currently living off of that. If there is some doubt, then we can say that in compliance with Catholic Social Teaching the minimum should be 3 sacks, which gives Ben a 50% raise. We could set it at 10 sacks per day, perhaps a "low" wage due to the added paperwork that Ben will cause Frank. We could split the increase 50/50 paying Ben 25 sacks per day. Frank might really hate the field work, and be willing to pay Ben 50 sacks a day if he can stay working the mill. In fact, Frank could pay Ben 197 sacks per day just to get out of the fields. Absent a market, how will you determine the proper wage for this very simplistic example? Consider that there might be a lot of "Franks" and only one Ben, so labor is limiting. Or there could be plenty of "Bens" and only one Frank, so capital is limiting. The answer is this: you can't make this determination, absent a market. YOU ARE NOT OMNISCIENT. This lack of omniscience is one of the fatal flaws of all left wing systems, and was first identified by the Austrian School of Economic theorists.

Now consider the Catholic system, which uses free market competition. In this system the "Franks" are continually considering their costs, markets, and the availability of "Bens". The "Bens" are continually evaluating their opportunities for advancement, living expenses, and are considering their motivations: wages, satisfaction of work, work conditions, and time involved. By this continuous search for better outcomes, information is conveyed via PRICING, whether for raw materials, finished goods, or wages. Therefore the system of free market competition always tends towards the optimal, and the participants in the system are not required to be omniscient, as something as simple as the price will direct their efforts where it is most needed. Resources are then said to be ALLOCATED via prices. For those familiar with numerical methods, the Catholic system is similar to a Nelder-Meade simplex optimizer. Compare this to the left wing systems which are little more than wild guesses, and will always result in the misallocation of resources.

The Calculation Problem: When an economic statist wishes to allocate capital and goods, as discussed above with the example of the Flour Planning Soviet, he is faced with what is termed the Calculation Problem. The calculation problem was demonstrated in the flour example above, but I will now more fully describe it. The Calculation Problem means that without a market it is impossible to determine what the price should be, what the quantity produced should be, and what wages should be. This is because we are not omniscient. The solution to this problem was

16

attempted by Trotsky, who said he would use international pricing to determine allocation. This is quite ironic as Trotsky wanted world-wide communism to destroy all markets, and his answer immediately raises the question: "If free markets work in international markets to set prices, work so well in fact that you will use them to direct your economy, then why not also use free markets?". So his attempt was a failure.

Interestingly it appears that Pesch was also trying to solve this problem. You may recall his answer: "the objective way to set prices is to ask everyone's opinion.". Pathetic.

The statement of the Calculation Problem was one of the greatest contributions to economic thought by the Austrian School, along with their dismantling of the Marxist Labor Theory of Value (discussed in the Appendix), and their inflation-induced business cycle theory.

Free Market Competition: A further consideration of free market competition is needed in the evaluation of economic systems, particularly with regards to the fallen nature of man. Again, we will consider an example. Chances are that if you open up your phone book you will find listed some 20 plumbers who are available to work on your plumbing problems. You as the local customer will most likely ask around when evaluating which plumber to use, check comments on the internet, as well as compare billing rates. Consider that this is rightly labeled a system of Subsidiarity, as the lowest level in society, the individual, is determining the allocation of plumbing services. The plumbers are said to be competing for your business, and a trade (i.e. plumbing vs. money) will only occur if you both can EXCHANGE VALUE FOR VALUE. If the plumber does a lousy job, chances are his reputation will be damaged, and he may even be forced out of business. THIS ABILITY FOR THE CONSUMER TO CHOOSE A PLUMBER, THE HALLMARK OF COMPETITION, IS CLEARLY SEEN TO BE A NATURAL

CHECK ON THE FALLEN NATURE OF ALL MEN, IN THIS CASE PLUMBERS. A plumber who wishes to eat will forgo lazy and/or corrupt practices because he knows he can not force consumers to put up with such practices. The importance of recognizing this concept can not be stressed enough.

Now consider a left wing system. In this case, we will consider a guild (also called a soviet). In this system, when you open the phone book, instead of seeing 20 plumbers listed, you will only see one listing labeled "Plumbers' Guild". You would call the guild and they would send you a plumber. You should by now instinctively see the problem of allocation of resources. Just how will the guild know the "right" billing rate to use? The Austrians identified this problem, as I mentioned earlier. This is the Calculation Problem. However, since the Austrian School is mostly agnostic, they have not identified another major flaw in left wing economic systems – the fallen nature of man. Suppose that the plumber assigned to you is the son of the Guild Master (or whatever he is called). Suppose he does a lousy job. What can you do? You could complain, but in the world I live in nothing would be done. The lousy plumber's son would be allowed to continue to (poorly) practice his craft. Furthermore, there is no guarantee that any of the plumbers would be qualified. Entrance into the guild could be awarded to family members, or the guild could require bribes. Original Sin will surely be a factor – as Catholics we know this. The Austrians, due to agnosticism, miss this key point about the advantage of competition.

For with competition, Man's fallen nature is naturally checked by the ability of the consumers to go somewhere else, motivated by poor service or an unfair price (which price is magically "guessed at" in the guild system), and more importantly <u>everyone</u> knows that poor service will lead to eventual bankruptcy. Furthermore, by limiting the power organizations hold over you (at the point of a gun), corruption is held in check. These are the clear advantages of a system of free market competition that are only revealed when we presuppose the fallen nature of man.

Usury: Usury is poorly understood today, and most people would erroneously say that usury is charging "too high" of an interest rate. This is wrong. Usury is charging for the use, AND ONLY THE USE, of money. Unfortunately the Church has been mostly silent about usury for around 300 years, during which times economies changed from serfs and or small scale operations, to large scale capital intensive industries. When usury was actively being debated, it mostly was in reference to usurers lending money to serfs for consumption purposes and indebting them, at times for life, with their usury charges. The Church rightfully worked to outlaw these practices. Later, some updates were made with St. Thomas and I believe Suarez in allowing certain fees to be charged in lending. I will attempt to apply certain of their concepts to our modern economic system.

First we begin with the definition, and study the conclusions. Usury is charging for the use of money only. However, receiving a share in the INCREASE in production is rightly called "your interest", or simply, interest. Usury is not interest. Consider a man who borrows money to start a business. If the business is profitable, the lender may rightly receive his interest in the production. Now if the business goes bust, in our usurious society the borrower is still required to pay what is now erroneously termed "interest". **For what is anyone's "interest" in zero production?** It is zero, and any such payment is properly called usury.

We therefore can see that usury is an offense against the Cardinal Virtue of Prudence, as I have shown that the interest in a non-productive loan is zero. That is reality. Therefore, I believe a fitting modern definition of usury (which still complies with Traditional Catholic teaching) is the charging of interest on a non-productive loan. People familiar with finance will understand when I also call it a non-self liquidating loan. I draw your

19

attention to the fact that the principle was not considered. The Church has always allowed lending, and the lender is due back his principle, even in a bankrupt business.

Equipped with this definition, we will now consider the idea that charging "too high" of an interest rate is usury. On one hand we will have the Federal Reserve bankers' guild loan money to member banks at 0.5% interest. On the other hand we will have a venture capitalist collecting 75% interest on a loan to a wildly successful start-up which has income well above the interest payment. The first case is usury. The second case is not.

Now Libertarians will say this does not matter (though I say anything imprudent is evil), since two free parties entered into an agreement, and therefore the terms must be respected. They will also discuss the time value of money, also called time preferences. Refuting this will allow me to introduce the second flaw of usury – Moral Hazard. It is true that the contract for usury is entered into freely, and that the interest rate reflects time preferences, but these are non-sequiturs. We could just the same discuss how the price is determined for a prostitute, e.g. consider the number of prostitutes, customers, and the involvement of pimps. Just because something makes superficial economic sense (I proved it was imprudent already, however) does not make it right, especially if usurious loans are used to deny reality and shield people from the consequences of poor planning, which is called Moral Hazard. Moral Hazard shields people and governments from the consequences of imprudence, and entering into a usurious loan freely does not remove this serious flaw.

Furthermore, from an economic perspective, we can see the other evil consequence of usury: It contributes to the business cycle. For as people go deeper and deeper into usurious debt, they consume the principle. Demand then is "artificial", and eventually it must come crashing down. Now an Austrian would say that the market will eventually balance things back out, but they must be careful in saying this, as we could say the same thing about inflation. And yet, every Austrian wants to go back to sound money and 100% reserve lending to PREVENT the business cycle. The same thing can be said about usury, that it must be outlawed to PREVENT the artificial demand from happening. Which, along with Moral Hazard, is the great evil of usury.

And a great evil it is. Next to inflation, I can not think of a greater economic evil than usury. In our society there are three examples of usury: government debt, except perhaps certain bonds backed by tolls, credit card debt, and now student loans after the ability to clear them through bankruptcy was removed. We shall consider government debt, and such consideration is probably unnecessary to prove my point.

Besides inflation, there has been no greater economic scourge upon mankind than government usury. It is the definition of Moral Hazard. It allows governments to rob their unborn citizens in order to gain political favor. It shields government from the consequences of their irresponsible spending. It has caused the death of millions. We consider the results of the French Revolution and its offspring, communism, to see how terrible usury really is.

The French Revolution was caused by the Sun King, whose policies and wars predated this horror by approximately one hundred years, though his successors contributed to the size of usurious debt. As a result of this massive usurious debt incurred by France, her economy was struggling during the reign of Louis XV. The regent of France, Phillipe d'Orleans appointed John Law as Controller General of Finances, who then started a central bank and the issuance of fiat paper money. The resulting misallocations resulted in a series of boom-busts cycles (see the Mississippi Bubble) which culminated in the severe depressions during Louis XVI's reign and the starvation of 1789, when bread prices rose 50-60%. If usury had been outlawed, these conditions would have been prevented.

A further demonstration of the evils of usury can be shown simply by considering this: that the Federal Reserve bankers' guild could not exist if it was not for usury.

There are a few more considerations about usury that I will briefly discuss. First is the question of whether mortgages and car loans are considered usurious. I will concentrate on mortgages, as the same concepts apply to car loans. On this question I am unsure. In one sense a mortgage is an extended form of a production loan, and hence is not usurious. The objection is obvious: Why then could not credit card debt to fund say a candy bar be considered a production loan? The answer to this must not be arbitrary, and in my opinion it is not. **The useful life of the product must be considered.** In other words, a house has a generally accepted useful life of 25 years, after which major maintenance is required including a new roof, painting, and carpet/flooring replacement. A candy bar has a useful life of mere minutes. After which the production is no longer in existence. In other words, the candy bar is consumed, the house is not.

Now I am unsure whether mortgages are usury, but the Moslems appear to have a solution to this, IF a home mortgage is indeed usury. First, it must be pointed out that certain Catholic historians, Belloc being the most notable, consider the Moslem sect to be an heresy that was heavily influenced by Christianity (though heavily distorted, I must say). As such certain of their practices can be considered time capsules of the earlier Church. Their doctrine opposing usury is one such practice. With that aside, I will discuss the key elements of their non-usurious system.

In this system, the bank and the home owner form what is rightfully called a trust, with ownership of the house placed in this trust. The owner buys a certain portion of this trust (the down payment), pays the trust rent, with the rental income distributed to

22

the owners of the trust. The home owner does not receive his share in cash, but instead it is used to slowly buy out the banker until the homeowner is sole owner of the trust. If the homeowner is forced out of the home due to loss of income, either it can continue to be rented to someone else, or it is liquidated, and the proceeds distributed in accordance to the shares of ownership.

Now the Sensus Catholicus indicates that this is pretty similar to a modern **non-recourse** mortgage, and therefore my personal opinion is that mortgages (non-recourse) are not usurious. I readily admit that further study of this is required, and in fact encouraged.

This can be seen also if we consider a rent-to-own agreement on a house. Certainly renting is not outlawed by the Church. In a rent-to-own agreement, the renter pays a fixed rate, and slowly acquires ownership in the house. Again, the Sensus Catholicus indicates that this is pretty similar to a modern non-recourse mortgage, and therefore my personal opinion is that mortgages (non-recourse) are not usurious.

Finally we should discuss the benefits of outlawing usury, something that those of the Austrian School should consider. If usury was outlawed, investment would no longer be directed towards consumption. Instead, investors would seek out opportunities where the investment had a REAL RETURN, by definition an exercise in prudence. In this way, the market would steer capital into PRODUCTION and CAPITAL FORMATION. One large problem of government usury bonds is that they rob capital from the productive economy. Outlawing usury will eliminate this problem.

Inflation: I will limit my discussion on inflation to fiat (i.e. unbacked) paper money. Though as a quick aside it must be noted that inflation in a gold-backed monetary system is possible (and has occurred in past times) with the discovery of a new large deposit of gold, though in modern times this can be considered extremely unlikely.

Inflation is therefore simply this: increasing the supply of fiat currency. In our current age this is usually in the form of electronic money, but most economists will still refer to this as "money printing" due to the historical practice of actually printing up more money.

Inflation is a great evil, and in fact can be considered THE great evil in economic systems. It has two consequences, first being a highly regressive tax on the poor and fixed pensioners, and second the misallocation of resources which occur during an inflation.

During an inflation of the money supply, let us consider the reality of what is happening, i.e. let us exercise prudence. Let us suppose that the Federal Reserve bankers' guild prints up $1 Trillion and buys up government usury bonds (the intertwining evils in this is mind numbing). The government ends up possessing $1 Trillion dollars, of which it may now purchase (or cause to be purchased through redistribution schemes) ACTUAL valuable goods and services. In sum, real value is consumed. This is what prudence indicates. But from whence does this real value originate? It comes from (loots) the purchasing power of the previously existing money. What is worse, the first consumers of the new money (rightly called "looters") will benefit as the devaluation will not be immediately evident. The responsible producers who save their money, or do not adjust their prices and thus consume their capital, will lose out. However the producers will still be better off (though suffer none-the-less) since they can eventually raise their prices, than the poor, who can not easily raise their wages. The poor, and those on fixed incomes and pensions will suffer the most as prices inevitably rise to reflect the devaluation. It is a great evil that rewards looting, punishes savers and producers, and drives the already poor into the depths of misery. The French Revolution and events leading up to it are evidence of this.

However, there is arguably an even greater evil involved, that of misallocation. Let us consider a builder of condo towers (a fitting example during this current Greater Depression). During an inflation, the developer will see his interest rates drop as the liquidity begins sloshing around the system, and at the same time he will see demand for his condos increase (he will be able to charge a higher price) as his customers also see their mortgage rates drop. His "potential" profits will increase dramatically. This is oftentimes called a boom. We can say that the market is now directing him to build more condos, or we can say it is allocating more resources to the condo developer. But since new resources have not suddenly become available, it can plainly be seen that the market IS NOW LYING TO HIM.

Also consider the buyers. Previously, before the inflation, they could not afford the condo. In other words, their productive output did not equal the costs of a condo, especially when considering their other expenses. Now, due to the omniscient decision of the Bankers' Guild, they can magically afford the condo, even though their production is the same as previously.

Bearing in mind the Virtue of Prudence, we must align ourselves with reality. No new resources are available, they buyers have not increased their production, and as long as the inflation lasts, resources will be severely wasted in unneeded construction. Prices will rise, and more resources will be allocated (redirected erroneously) to supporting industries. Furthermore, according to DePrisco's Law, a demand curve pushed out by inflation will become inelastic to lower prices. Therefore, business owners who forecast higher sales will be mislead, because dropping the price will have little effect. They will erroneously increase production assuming the demand will be there, meanwhile they will see their own costs increase in price.

This must eventually end in what is called the bust as the limitation in resources eventually becomes obvious. This bust is usually initiated when the central bank, in our case the Federal Reserve bankers' guild, is forced to end the inflation due to political pressures resulting from the rising prices. And the bust can be severe, so severe that it can destroy a country.

This next point must be firmly grasped if one is to understand how economies work: THE EVIL IS IN THE BOOM. The bust, also called a recession or a depression, is a corrective measure by which resources are salvaged and an economy is restored to reality, albeit the economy will be much poorer due to the extreme waste inherent in a boom. For this reason (the revealed degraded condition of the economy after the boom, which we can call "fessing up" or "admitting the truth", i.e. being prudent) the recession is fought tooth and nail, usually with another wave of inflation. We are currently witnessing this phenomena during the Greater Depression.

It may be that the best that can be done with wasted condo towers is that they are demolished and the copper recovered. Such is the boom-bust cycle.

Sadly some conservative Republicans, who tend to favor a Catholic economic system, will support fiat currency and the bankers' guild. Their reasoning is as follows:
Capitalism (which I have called "free market competion") = good (This is true)
Banking = capitalism (not necessarily true, only if it is not usurious. Banks exist in fascist systems and capitalism can exist without banking. Banking is merely a tool, syndicating the money of savers so that it can be loaned out.)
The Federal Reserve bankers' guild is part of banking. (True, but it is usurious and inflationary)
Federal Reserve = good. (Patently false).

The answer to the boom-bust cycles of inflation can be realized with two possible systems. The preferred method would be to outlaw fractional reserve banking, whereby banks lend out more than they have on deposit via the machinations of the Federal Reserve, which is by definition inflationary, while at the same time backing money 100% with gold. This eliminates inflation to a maximum of the production of new gold, which is minuscule in percentage terms. We call this the gold standard.

The second system may be the only politically possible system. That is the green back system whereby the government issues the currency, again coupled with the elimination of fractional reserve banking, i.e. banks could only lend out the deposits on hand. It is debatable whether the money supply would be fixed, or whether it would increase by an unchangeable 1% each year to accommodate increases in population and productivity. Such a 1% annual increase would be "good enough". This increase would be fixed and predictable, and the increase in money supply would be deposited in the US Treasury and thus can be considered a tax.

Those familiar with the Austrian School will probably cringe, and likewise Catholics who truly accept Original Sin will be wary, as the temptation would be strong (and perhaps irresistible) for the government to discover some loop hole to allow them to print. Prudence would dictate that the former solution of using gold is preferable.

The only reason I introduce the greenback option is that I am unsure of the effects of instantly making the dollar convertible to gold. Some calculations show that the price of gold would sky rocket to $10,000 per ounce or more. If this was the extent of the effect, then it would not be a problem. However such a massively deflationary move would cause a severe depression, so severe that it may not be politically possible. A sincere Austrian must admit, however, that the green back solution coupled with the elimination of fractional reserve banking would be a vast improvement.

<u>Unions and the Living Wage</u> Another concept that has been severely distorted is that of the Living Wage. The Living Wage doctrine first and foremost is a concern of Catholic EMPLOYERS (not governments). Such a Catholic must evaluate the needs in his community for establishing a just wage level. Now the problem arises in large corporations where there is not one Catholic owner, but a large number of managers. In this case Original Sin can invade and the workers suffer.

Most modern Catholics, in this case of large industries, would equate the Living Wage doctrine with minimum wage laws. Nothing could be further from the Truth. In fact, Pope Leo XIII clearly rejects this in *Rerum Novarum*: "In these and similar questions, however - such as, for example, the hours of labor in different trades, the sanitary precautions to be observed in factories and workshops, etc. - **in order to supersede undue interference on the part of the State**, especially as circumstances, times, and localities differ so widely, it is advisable that recourse be had to societies or boards such as We shall mention presently, or to some other mode of safeguarding the interests of the wage-earners; the State being appealed to, should circumstances require, for its sanction and protection."

So the problem still exists of how to best guarantee a Living Wage without involving "undue interference on the part of the State". The reader should also recall that there is no "right" answer for the allocation of resources, or the allocation of gains to capital (the "Franks") and labor (the "Bens"). The answer to this problem is to utilize collective bargaining, i.e. to utilize Catholic labor unions. These labor unions MUST follow the restrictions laid down by St. Pius X, previously sited, and follow the religious intentions also put forth by Pope Leo XIII: "workers' associations ought to be so constituted and so governed as to furnish the most suitable and most convenient means to attain the object proposed, which consists in this, that the individual members of the association secure, so far as is possible, an increase in the goods of body, of soul, and of property," yet it is clear that "moral and religious perfection ought to be regarded as their principal goal, and that their social organization as such ought above all to be directed completely by this goal."[22] For "when the regulations of associations are founded upon religion, the way is easy toward establishing the mutual relations of the members, so that peaceful living together and prosperity will result. RN"

After reading the Encyclical Singulari Quadam, it is obvious that no Catholic can belong to modern labor unions. I wish to stress especially to those who support Free Markets not to rush to judgment on the idea of collective bargaining. Our current unions are little more than criminal rackets, and need a major reform, even going back to the drawing board. With that in mind, I propose the following guidelines for establishing a Catholic labor movement:

1. The unions must be Catholic. The members must never support politicians who are in favor of such vile practices such as abortion or homosexual "marriage".

2. Unions, in recognition on the Doctrine of Subsidiarity, must be local. The "nationals" must be abolished.

3. Unions should concern themselves with collective bargaining over wages and safe, humane working conditions only. They should also act to represent a worker during a dispute or disciplinary hearing.

4. Unions should not have any authority to bargain over "work rules". The insistence on the "work rules" rackets comes from the flawed economic theory (similar to "stimulus") that you must "make work" for employees. For example, there is the insistence that if workers accidentally trip a circuit breaker, then work must shut down and an electrician called out (with 4 hour minimum pay and overtime) to reset the breaker, rather than the worker, say a carpenter, merely plugging into a separate plug and resetting the breaker. This derives from the flawed notion that you need to "create" more work for the laborers (as opposed to reality – you are raising costs). Work responsibility rests with the employers and is set by the job description.

5. The same holds true for the sick leave/overtime rackets. Calling in sick (and this gets pretty organized in practice, with workers taking turns) to drive up overtime should be called what it truly is: stealing. Sick leave is a benefit for those who are truly sick. Again, this policy should be set by the employer.

6. For reasons of a serious conflict of interest, public unions should be outlawed. Again, it does not serve the common good to have the public

unions help elect "their guy" into office, which politician will then sit across from them at the bargaining table from whence he agrees to the looting of the taxpayer.

7.   Right to Work laws are required. No one should be forced to join the union, the Popes have spoken. The competition between union and non-union is healthy in keeping the former honest. Some will argue that there will be free-loaders on the union who don't pay dues. But ask yourself why there is a need for huge dues in the first place. It is because the "nationals" take a huge cut, and the union management loots from the worker. An honest assessment would come to the conclusion that the union dues should be small, so that most would be happy to pay it in exchange for union representation in disputes. In other words, unions should trade value for value: representation for a modest fee.

In exchange for these reforms, the unions would have the protection of the law. Workers would be free to form and join a union, and be protected from discrimination by the employer. If the reforms were enacted, then the unions would be a great benefit to the company, whereby the worker would feel that his needs are being properly represented. Furthermore, as one very anti-union individual confided to me, if unions didn't exist, they would have to be invented, as negotiating with 1,000 individuals vs. agreeing to one contract would waste a lot of time and effort.

With these reforms in place, a true Catholic labor movement would be established. And such a movement would utilize collective bargaining as opposed to "undue interference by the State" to determine the just wage. Furthermore, it would be religious, such that the union would look at the company they bargain with as a valued client deserving justice, a union where the president meets with the company and says, "We want you to succeed. We want to complete the project by the deadline and come in under budget."

Monopolies A monopoly is a situation whereby an entity is the sole owner, or has sole coercive power, in an economic or government arrangement. All men on the right of the spectrum oppose monopolies as they preclude or severely limit the possibility of competition. Most men of the left oppose private monopoly, but are strong proponents for government monopolies, either guilds (soviets), syndicates, or economic bureaus, or in the case of socialism, government monopolistic ownership.

Monopolies are bad because they prevent or limit competition. They can arise due to four causes:

1. Natural conditions. For example it is economically impossible to have three parallel water supply systems, with three water companies competing for you business. This is properly called a natural monopoly.

2. A monopoly could be established by law, for example via licensing in the private sector, whereby only one firm is granted a license in a certain field. Cable TV was an example of this, though Satellite TV has risen to compete against it. Government is the obvious legal monopoly, and economic boards such as guilds, syndicates, and soviets are another.

3. A monopoly can exist due to regulatory compliance costs, whereby it is difficult for a small company to enter into a business because it does not have enough financial resources to hire the lawyers, accountants, and engineers needed just to stay in regulatory compliance. When large firms lobby to establish regulatory burdens, this process is termed "rent seeking".

4. Standardization: An early inventing firm in an industry can become a monopoly because their patented technology becomes the industry standard. The Micosoft Windows Operating System is an example of this.

Monopolies are evil because they limit competition, as I previously stated. The prime question is what one is to do about them. As for legal monopolies and those resulting due to regulations, the answer is to avoid creating them in the first place. With that being said, I will limit my further discussion to natural monopolies and those arising from standardization.

Even the most right wing Libertarian recognizes that natural monopolies are not optimal. The question again is what to do with them. For this problem, I again support what I call the "good enough" approach, which is the utility board. This is the solution chosen in most communities, and involves a government board that approves rates. The rates are set to guarantee a reasonable profit, and enough retained earnings to provide for capital expenditures.

The Austrian approach would be to let the monopolies operate unmolested. I disagree with this, but in fairness they will readily admit this is not a perfect solution, and competition would be preferable. Again, the utility board appears to work acceptably, and my utility bills appear "reasonable". I am sure that having competing water utility companies would result in better service and lower rates, but that is not to be.

The other example of monopolies that we need to address is that of standardization. For this problem (and indeed it is a problem) I support the use of anti-competitive practice legislation. I base my understanding of economics on the teaching about Original Sin by the Catholic Church, and I support efforts to increase competition. We can look at two examples.

First, there is the break-up of the AT&T monopoly. That has been a huge success. If this had not occurred, then imagine what would have happened with cell phones. Since competing companies would not be able to tie into AT&T landlines, cellphone companies would by default be limited to one – AT&T. However, due to the break-up, now AT&T must compete with other companies, and as a result prices have fallen dramatically. Again, competition is a good thing.

The other example is the Microsoft operating system. Microsoft runs a computer monopoly, and their operating system has been buggy and has had security flaws. Also, it has a habit of "calling home to mama", something that I don't accept. Fortunately it appears that Android will make the jump to PCs sometime soon, as it is already in Smartphones and now Tablets. Apple iOS is also a strong competitor.

I believe that most computer experts would agree that breaking up the Microsoft operating system monopoly and replacing it with an open system would be very beneficial. Then Microsoft could concentrate on applications, something they appear to be good at. I personally like the Linux operating system, but it has been a chore to get vendors to provide drivers for it, and the application side has some pretty significant holes in it. If the computer industry would standardize on an open system like Linux, we would have a much improved computer industry.

These are two good examples that support my position – that efforts to increase competition are prudent actions.

Free Trade In order to have an intelligent discussion on Free Trade, both sides – the Free Traders and those who support tariffs – must agree on a given fact. For a *given system*, a policy of Free Trade will be the most optimal and provide the most benefit to the most people. This is a fact.

Let us consider an example. Let us suppose China makes efforts to increase their productive capacity by subsidizing industries and fixing their exchange rate, all in the context of a free trade regime; in this case the *system* will be China and the USA. By the fact above, the system will be optimized. In this case, 100's of millions of Chinese will improve their lives while millions of Americans will lose. Taken as a whole, the system will improve as a result.

And therein lies the problem. I am not Chinese, and beyond the minimal interest of human decency, I could care less about China. However, I am an American, and I care greatly about the USA.

Now the argument put forth by Bastiat in favor of Free Trade, was to ask "If tariffs are so good, why not have the different political counties/States also have tarriffs?" Again, we must define the system. In this case, the system should be the USA. So within the system, free trade is optimal. China is **outside** the USA system, therefore allowing their policies to run without any regulation has had a negative impact on the USA. I have come to the conclusion that some regulation of trade is beneficial to the USA.

Before exploring tariffs, I would be remiss if I did not mention an example where Free Trade proved to be very beneficial. In the late 70's, the car industry in the USA was run by one company, the UAW. By that time the quality of UAW produced cars had been reduced to laughable levels. US cars were junk. Sure there were three or four "brands" (e.g. Ford, Chrysler, GM), but it was really one industry run by the UAW. Into this horrible situation the Japanese entered with their products, primarily Honda and Toyota. These high quality, reasonably priced cars utterly overwhelmed the "comparable" high priced junk produced by the UAW. Because of this competition, major changes were made in Detroit, and US companies started fighting back against the UAW. Eventually, due to the threat of tariffs, the Japanese started building their car factories in the USA – a good thing.

So a regulation of trade needs to consider both ends. First, it must optimize the system, in this case the USA ONLY, and second, it must still allow competition. My solution would be an across-the-board flat tariff of 10%. It is somewhat arbitrary, but still based on my personal observations. I would certainly pay 10% more for a Japanese brand during the late 70's, but the 10% rate is about the profit rate of many companies and would give a sizable advantage to QUALITY US producers. Coupled with a FAIR tax (discussed in the next section), foreign producers would be put at a severe disadvantage.

The tariff must be flat. We live in a fallen world, and there would be pressure on government to support "favored" industries, such as the UAW infested car industry in the 70s. By keeping the tariff flat, this power to corrupt the economy would be eliminated.

Furthermore, one must consider that we must pay taxes anyway. Therefore, why not trade a flat 10% tariff for say a lower FAIR tax rate?

<u>Alms</u> Go into any sizable US city and you are sure to run into a Catholic hospital (or many). Did you ever wonder why this is so? This might appear puzzling to some people, and this puzzlement is proof of the success of the campaign by Progressives to spread The Big Lie – that government is responsible for relief of the poor. I will state here again what the Pope has declared:
""it becomes a duty to give to the indigent out of what remains over. "Of that which remaineth, give alms."(14) It is a duty, **not of justice** (save in extreme cases), but of Christian charity - **a duty not enforced by human law**." -- RN

Therefore in a properly ordered society the government has no involvement in the relief of the poor, except in extreme cases, e.g. Hurricane Katrina (and we can debate how effective that was). The relief of the poor is reserved to the Church, and to the parishioners of said Church, who provide alms to Catholic Relief Societies and also to parish efforts. In this way, a poor man must take responsibility for his actions, and a drunk will have to talk to the pastor in order to receive aid.

Now you understand why our forefathers saw to the establishment of a Catholic medical system which was heavily involved in providing medical services to the poor.

For the government does a poor job at relief. Eventually it will establish a subculture of able bodied looters who wait at home for their "check" and will build up in numbers such that their votes will keep the looters in power. Eventually they will grow to outnumber the producers and the system will collapse. In the USA, 47% of the population does not pay any Federal Income Tax. That number will grow as the number of Social Security recipients balloons. The few remaining producers will hold back, or go black market, and we are only a few years (months?) away from the inevitable collapse.

Which is why the prudent system is a system of Church sponsored relief, which as an added benefit allows the parishioners to acquire Gracious merit. However, most Americans now take for granted that the government is supposed to redistribute wealth, which is why our government usury debt is closing in on $16 Trillion at the time of this writing. ($20 Trillion – second edition).

ANALYSIS OF ALTERNATIVE SYSTEMS

Policitcal Spectrum in the Economic Sphere: In order to proceed further in my presentation of Catholic subsidiarity in the Economic Sphere, it is necessary to define the terms, specifically left wing and right wing. I shall divide up the economic systems into a continuum, from minimal government power, to total government power. This is for the economic sphere only. Below are my terms, and these should be considered as existing on a continuum:

Right Wing
> Anarcho-Capitalism: No government. All problems are handled by the private sector, including private security forces and private boards of arbitration.

> Catholic Subsidiarity: A government based on subsidiarity and free market competition. The government provides

police power, a criminal court system, a civil court system limited to settling disputes, a deeds office to establish and maintain property rights and transfers, and running certain monopolies (e.g. roads) where efficiency dictates its use.

Republican: Limited government, but more involved with the economy. Certain Republicans support the Federal Reserve banking guild and promote the use of government to support business.

Left Wing:
Democrat: Supports a more active government, some redistribution of wealth, but still allows private property.

Distributist: Popular with a minority of Traditional Catholics. Small industries are organized into governing guilds. Large industries are organized into highly regulated syndicates (i.e, it is the corporatist/mercantile system) including labor union and government representation. Disputes are settled by the government. Private ownership of property is allowed. Distribution of wealth is utilized via taxation to provide "property" to small businesses.

Fascist/National Socialist: Highly regulated private ownership of the means of production, with heavy government direction. Theoretically differing from Distributism by the involvement of government in the lower levels of the guild/syndicate system.

Socialist: Private personal property, but government ownership of the means of production.

Communist: No private property.

From the above the USA would be considered as having a left wing economic system with a mix of distributism (banking, doctors, and lawyers), Fascism (EPA, OSHA, EEOC, NLRB) and socialism (Social Security, Amtrak).

I will begin by looking at objections from the right.

<u>Anarcho-Capitalist:</u> First there are the anarcho-capitalists. Their position is basic: no government. However, this group can be further broken up into two groups, the agnostics and the Catholics.

The agnostics deny Original Sin. They believe that man unfettered by government will naturally evolve a society of peaceful coexistence, paradoxically basing their same premise on that of the socialists – a utopia is possible. I am a Catholic, and through revelation, and from my own observations in life, I know that Original Sin exists. I will waste no more time with this group.

The second group of Anarcho-capitalists are the Catholics. This group provides a reasonable argument: That indeed Original Sin exists, therefore giving the government ANY power will lead to an evil outcome. I sympathize with this position; it rests on a sound premise, however the conclusions are flawed.

I reject their conclusions based on two reasons. First, history proves time and again that when society breaks down, the region will come under the governance of a "war lord". Any effort by the citizens to oppose the "war lord" must be a de facto government, and so the anarcho-capitalist system can not emerge. We can look to history, perhaps the best example being the rise of feudalism after the decline of Rome, to see this play out.

Second, as Catholics it is beneficial to consult with the Bible. The only time that I am aware of where God set up a government, it was a confederation of sovereign States (tribes) headed by a weak

central government, which weakness is indicated by its title –
Judges. So the constitutional form of limited government has
some strong support.

Catholic Anarcho-Capitalism only occupies a small number of
Catholics. Anyone requiring a further refutation is urged to
consult the Encyclical by Pope Leo XIII entitled *LIBERTAS*.

Ayn Rand: Obviously not an "alternate system", but the
popularity of her amongst Catholics deserves some commentary.

Why then is Rand popular with Catholics, especially her Opus
Atlas Shrugged? The reason is simple: Ayn Rand's arguments
were Catholic. There were two fatal flaws, which I shall discuss,
but the educated Catholic reading this book should be able to spot
Aristotle and even Aquinas in the following quotes, because Rand
based her arguments on Aristotle, and was an admirer of St.
Thomas Aquinas.

"Destroyers seize gold and leave to its owners a counterfeit pile of
paper. This kills all **objective standards** and delivers men into the
arbitrary power of an arbitrary setter of values. Gold was an
objective value, an equivalent of wealth produced. Paper is a
mortgage on wealth that does not exist, backed by a gun aimed at
those who are expected to produce it. Paper is a check drawn by
legal looters upon an account which is not theirs: upon the **virtue**
of the victims. Watch for the day when it bounces, marked:
'Account Overdrawn.'"

"The fence you have been straddling....is the coward's formula
contained in the sentence: 'But we don't have to go to extremes!'
The extreme you have always struggled to avoid is the recognition
that **reality** is final, **that A is A and that the truth is true**. A
moral code impossible to practice, a code that demands
imperfection or death, has taught you to dissolve all ideas in fog,
to permit no firm definitions, to regards any concept as

approximate and any rule of conduct as elastic, to hedge on any principle, to compromise on any value, to take the middle of any road."

Read the next quote with the Obama campaign for "change" in mind: "As they proclaim that the only requirement for running a factory is the ability to turn the cranks of the machines, and blank out the question of who created the factory -- so they proclaim that there are no **entities**, that nothing exists but motion, and blank out the fact that motion presupposes the thing which moves, that without the concept of **entity**, there can be no such concept of 'motion'. As they proclaim their right to consume the unearned, and blank out the question of who's to produce it -- so they proclaim that there is no **law of identity**, that nothing exists but change and blank out that the fact that change presupposes the concepts of what changes, from what and to what, that without the law of identity no such concept as "change" is possible..."

"The **law of identity** does not allow you to have your cake and eat it, too. The **law of causality** does not permit you to eat your cake before you have it. But if you drown both laws in the blanks of your mind, if you pretend to yourself and to others that you don't see -- then you can try to proclaim your right to eat your cake today, and mine tomorrow, you can preach that the way to make cake is to eat it first, before you bake it, that the way to produce is to start by consuming (Iron Law --jad), that all wishers have an equal claim to all things, since nothing is **caused** by anything."

Indeed these are CATHOLIC arguments. However, Ayn Rand held to two premises that are in error: She was an atheist and denied that God existed, and she denied Original Sin. Because of this, she is a tragic figure, a natural Catholic who probably died unrepentant. May God have mercy on her soul.

We see tantalizing evidence that she was close. She wrote *Atlas Shrugged* which presented a society of Fallen Man. And yet she concludes in the famous John Galt speech that the belief in Original Sin was the cause of our troubles. She also defined two enemies, the Looters of Material, i.e. leftists, and the Looters of the Spirit, i.e. those who acknowledge that God exists. However, notably she gives no example in the whole book about the Looters of the Spirit. She originally tried, and this is striking as she had to abandon it, as the following quote reveals: "In an introduction, Leonard Peikoff mentions that Ayn Rand had a priest for a character who took confessions from James Taggart, Dagny's brother. This character was cut out, because, as Ayn Rand said, **she couldn't make him convincing**."

Sad. Perhaps the merciful Lord used her admiration of St. Thomas as a means towards a death-bed conversion, but we shall never know in this life.

Republican/Democrat: I put these political parties on my economic continuum merely as "buckets" in an effort to orientate the reader. There isn't really a hard-and-fast rule for their economic systems (hence the continuum), and therefore I will not comment on it any further, except to say that Republicans are more-or-less on the "Right" in my system, and Democrats are on the "Left". I shall now consider the arguments of the leftists.

Socialism: As previously stated, Socialism is a system whereby the government owns all productive property, but private property (e.g. houses and cars) still exists. Therefore a private company does not exist under this system. Furthermore, and fatal, a market does not exist as the government will set the prices.

Socialism suffers from three fatal flaws. First, as the Austrians pointed out, there is no market available to allocate resources. Production is set by government fiat and you are faced with the Calculation Problem. Therefore, a major premise must be that the government possesses god-like powers, in this case omniscience, that allows it to set prices and production targets. This is, prima facie, ridiculous. Men are not gods, so the government will be wrong in most (all?) cases. The result will be a misallocation of resources and an extremely dysfunctional economy. History has shown this by many examples.

Second, this system presupposes that men will produce to their ability. But in this system, more work will result in punishment, not reward. This was pointed out by Ayn Rand. The harder you work, the more work will be allotted to you. Furthermore, your reward is contingent on the benevolence of your government masters. Working harder does not guarantee advancement, and in fact might be an indication that you would cause trouble. So those who produce in a socialist economy will quickly learn that the pragmatic course is to "throttle back". As the Russians used to quip: "They pretend to pay us so we pretend to work".

Third, all leftists have as their premise that Original Sin does not exist. They believe that a workers' utopia is possible. As Catholics we reject this. The prudent economic system must presuppose Original Sin, and the Socialist system does just the opposite. It is not prudent.

Communism: Communism is differentiated from Socialism in that private property is completely illegal. The arguments against Socialism equally apply to Communism, and as such I will not comment further on Communism.

Distributism: I have saved my discussion on Distributism for last as it must necessarily be longer. This is due to the fact that some call Distributism the "Catholic" economic system. This is not the case, as I will show. Furthermore, as an aside, Fascism and Nazism are theoretically only a more militarized and regulated form of Distributism, so I will not discuss them separately. The same arguments will apply.

First, what is Distributism? Most Distributists will not be able to answer you as they will present mere "goals", such as the widespread ownership of property and small farms. There is an obsession with farming: organic farms, sustainable farming techniques, and CSA (community supported agriculture). For the record, I have and value a few acres, have participated in a CSA, and shop from farmers markets and a produce coop. But I am free to do this in a free market.

They also talk about fantasies of local Catholic communities of small farmers gathering at Smitty's pub for a smoke and a sampling of the locally brewed ale, with discussion centered around some Catholic topic led by a graduate in Liberal Arts. Of course the local guild masters, mindful of their Catholic duties, will support those Liberal Arts graduates with a stipend for their scholarly discussions at Smitty's. Such is the Distributist. For the second edition I have coined a descriptive term for them: Hobbiton LARPers.

Beyond that, Distributism is an actual system with some very troubling aspects. From my research, particularly of Belloc, the Distributist system is the following: First, local craftsman, e.g. plumbers, are coerced at the point of a gun to join a guild (which in Russia is called a soviet). The guild is government sponsored, and thus anyone trying to do business outside of the guild will be rounded up by dark windowed Ford Expeditions and hauled off to spend 10 years in the rape rooms of the Federal penitentiary. This is a detail that a Distributist will not reveal.

Second, for larger industries, syndicates of labor, "owners", and government will be formed, though the inclusion of government is usually mentioned in passing. In Fascism it is explicit. In the Distributist system we are told only that government will arbitrate when there is disagreement. Again, attempts to do business outside of the syndicate system will result in imprisonment.

Third, there will be a goal to increase ownership of "property" by all citizens. This will be done by an exorbitant property tax, which proceeds will be given to the rest of the citizenry as subsidies to buy "property". In a sense the victim of theft will be forced at the point of a gun to load his property in the getaway car, though in this case the looter will stay and the owner will be forced to "getaway".

It must be mentioned again that the Distributists seem fixated on setting up small farms, and even have the number of acres determined: 150 acres. How they arrive at that, I don't know, because making a living on anything short of a section of land is very difficult, and the loss of the economies of scale for such a small farm are insurmountable, except for where niche markets exist. As small farmers are quick to quip: "Behind every successful small farmer is a wife who works in town". I also can't imagine the response of New York City dwellers being told they need to move out to 150 acres of range land in Western Oklahoma.

Lastly, ownership of large farms, or large businesses will be illegal. Again, at the point of a gun.

This then is what I believe an objective observer knowledgeable about Distributism would call an honest definition. Let us analyze this system.

We must look at the claim that Distributism is Catholic. Recently I have found evidence to back this claim, in particular in the Encyclical *DIVINI REDEMPTORIS* written in 1937, and to a lesser extent in
QUADRAGESIMO ANNO written in 1931.

First some background. Prior to the publication of QA in 1931, the governing document for Catholic Social teaching was *RERUM NOVARUM* written by Pope Leo XIII. As I have previously alluded to, this Encyclical is a defense of private property and the free market system. So much so that Catholics noticed this fact, and Pope Pius XI had to comment on it in *QA*: "Yet since there are some who calumniate the Supreme Pontiff, and the Church herself, as if she had taken and were still taking the part of the rich against the non-owning workers - certainly no accusation is more unjust than that - and since Catholics are at variance with one another concerning the true and exact mind of Leo, it has seemed best to vindicate this, that is, the Catholic teaching on this matter from calumnies and safeguard it from false interpretations." *QA*

I can only assume he is referencing *RERUM NOVARUM* as this is the topic of *QA*, but Pope Leo XIII also has this troubling section (troubling to leftists, and particularly guild socialist, i.e. Distributists) in *LONGINQUA*: "Let them, however, never allow this to escape their memory: that whilst it is proper and desirable to assert and secure the rights of the many, yet this is not to be done by a violation of duty; and that these are very important duties; not to touch what belongs to another; to allow every one to be **free in the management of his own affairs**; not to hinder any one **to dispose of his services when he please and where he please**."

In the passing of time between the reign of Pope Leo XIII and 1931, a guild banking system had been established in the form of the private Federal Reserve in the USA, and this guild had allowed a runaway inflation in the "Roaring Twenties", which boom eventually resulted in a bust starting in 1929. This is not surprising, as a guild does not have the god-like power of omniscience to determine the price, i.e. the interest rate. But I get ahead of myself.

This bust, as opposed to the bust in 1921 discussed by Thomas Woods, was fought tooth-and-nail by the government by the establishment of a syndicate system (the New Deal) and by further money printing. These government and guild activities resulted in a Depression by 1931, the time of *QA*, and more importantly caused a further collapse by 1937, the time of the writing of *DIVINI REDEMPTORIS*. Pope Pius mentions this in *QA*: "99.

Important indeed have the changes been which both the economic system and Socialism have undergone since Leo XIII's time. 100. That, in the first place, the whole aspect of economic life is vastly altered, is plain to all"

That is the background. We will now confront the writings of Pope Pius XI. First, there was QA, written in 1931, about the time that the Depression was in full swing, but far from the nadir later in the decade. In *QA* Pope Pius XI gives us the definition of Subsidiarity and further condemns Socialism, to the point that he declared a Catholic could not be a Socialist. For these, we are grateful.

However, also in the Encyclical he mentions the changes in the economy (he must be talking about the Depression) and asks Catholics to consider the corporatist system. Historians have concluded that he is referring to Italian Fascism, as mentioned by von Mises. I will quote in length Pope Pius XI: "Recently, as all know, there has been inaugurated a special system of syndicates and corporations of the various callings which in view of the theme of this Encyclical it would seem necessary to describe here briefly and comment upon appropriately."

"The associations, or corporations, are composed of delegates from the two syndicates (that is, of workers and employers) respectively of the same industry or profession and, as true and proper organs and institutions of the State, they direct the syndicates and coordinate their activities in matters of common interest toward one and the same end. 94. Strikes and lock-outs are forbidden; if the parties cannot settle their dispute, **public authority intervenes.** 95. Anyone who gives even slight attention to the matter will easily see what are the obvious advantages in the system We have thus summarily described: The various classes work together peacefully, socialist organizations and their activities are repressed, and a special magistracy exercises a governing authority."

"........Anyone is free to join a syndicate **or not**, and only within these limits can this kind of syndicate be called free; for syndical dues and special assessments are exacted of absolutely all members of every specified calling or profession, whether they are workers or employers; likewise all are bound by the labor agreements made by the legally recognized syndicate." QA

Two observations are evident. First, Pope Pius XI is "presenting" this system for consideration. That is clear from the context, and later in D.R. he outright states it: "Or of those Catholic industrialists who even to this day have shown themselves hostile to a labor movement that We Ourselves **recommended**?" Clearly at this time a Catholic is not required to establish this system.

Second, and very important, the last paragraph states that workers and owners are free to join, **OR NOT.** So at this point Pope Pius XI is not in opposition to Pope Leo XIII, especially *LONGINQUA*, which bears repeating: "Let them, however, never allow this to escape their memory: that whilst it is proper and desirable to assert and secure the rights of the many, yet this is not to be done by a violation of duty; and that these are very important duties; not to touch what belongs to another; to allow every one to be **free in the management of his own affairs**; not to hinder any one **to dispose of his services when he please and where he please**."

I do not have a problem with a voluntary syndicate system (and a system where one may choose not to participate must be labeled "voluntary"), except for the monopoly powers it would entail. But history has shown that cartels quickly collapse when they are forced to compete against non-members.

And I have personally witnessed a situation where a voluntary "syndicate" was successful. In this case I was involved in a project in a Right-to-Work State and noticed a Union contractor. I inquired about this to the client, and was told that they preferred using hall labor because they always got quality craftsman. I also found out that certain "make-work" requirements, i.e. work rules, were waived by the hall. For example, craftsman were allowed to run the man-lift and were not required to call out an equipment operator to run it. Note that this was only possible in the context of a Right-to-Work State. Due to competition the hall was forced to send only quality craftsman, work rules were relaxed, and the scrubs were probably sent to closed-shop projects. Too bad for them.

If this was the extent of it, then there would be no issue, as it is impossible to run the Distributist system unless producers are FORCED into a guild. But later during the nadir of the economic collapse in 1937 (caused paradoxically by a banking guild), Pope Pius XI goes further and contradicts himself and opposes the Encyclicals of Pope Leo XIII. I believe the influence of Pesch is clearly seen, and Thomas Storck directly attributed these ideas to him: "It was to the thought of Pesch and his disciples that Pope Pius XI turned to in composing his monumental encyclical *Quadragesimo Anno* (1931)" The results are also evident in D.R.:

"53. It happens all too frequently, however, under the salary system, that individual employers are helpless to ensure justice unless, with a view to its practice, they organize institutions the object of which **is to prevent competition** incompatible with fair treatment for the workers. Where this is true, it is the **duty** of contractors and employers to support and promote such necessary organizations as normal instruments enabling them to fulfill their obligations of justice. ....If, therefore, We consider the whole structure of economic life, as We have already pointed out in Our Encyclical *Quadragesimo Anno*, the reign of mutual collaboration between justice and charity in social-economic relations **can only be achieved** by a body of professional and inter-professional organizations, built on solidly Christian foundations, working together to effect, under forms adapted to different places and circumstances, what has been called the Corporation ." D.R.

This one section of D.R. then allows the Distributist to claim they promote the "Catholic" system. Since it exists, their claim can not be called dishonest. However, it is erroneous to make this claim.

First, how is a Catholic supposed to understand this statement, especially when the Pope states that "the reign of mutual collaboration between justice and charity in social-economic relations **can only be achieved"** by this system? I argue that determining whether an economic system is optimal can not be called a situation of "Faith and Morals", and thus can't be infallible, but for the sake of argument, I will assume that it does concern "Faith and Morals". Given this assumption, what then are we to conclude, that this is infallible?

Let us consult Ott: "With regard to the doctrinal teaching of the Church it must be well noted that not all the assertions of the Teaching Authority of the Church on questions of Faith and morals are infallible and consequently irrevocable. Only those are infallible which emanate from General Councils representing the whole episcopate, and the Papal Decisions Ex Cathedra (cf. D 1839). The **ordinary and usual form of the Papal teaching activity is not infallible**. Further, the **decisions of the Roman Congregations** (Holy Office, Bible Commission) are **not infallible**. Nevertheless **normally they are to be accepted with an inner assent** which is based on the high supernatural authority of the Holy See (assensus internus supernaturalis, assensus religiosus). The so-called "silentium obsequiosum." that is "reverent silence," does not generally suffice. By way of exception, the **obligation of inner agreement may cease** if a competent expert, after a renewed scientific investigation of all grounds, arrives at the positive conviction that the **decision rests on an error**."

I present to you that we have an even better reason to conclude that Pope Pius XI's decision rests on error than the competent expert (though they exist, see the Austrian School), we have history itself. It is well known that the Italian Fascist system was a complete failure economically as well as the related German Nazi system. Both ended in inflation, debt, and a failing economy. We have an even greater example in Franco's Spain, which must be called a Catholic government (no excuse of occultist Nazis here), who in 1958 abandoned the corporatist system, because **it did not work**. Over the next decade Spain's economy was systematically returned to a free market system and the positive results were striking.

Furthermore we have the case of dueling Encyclicals. First we have Pope Pius XI opposing Pope Leo XIII, and we have Pope Pius XI opposing himself. Which one is infallible? That Pope Pius XI disagreed with Pope Leo XIII he himself admits: "You know, Venerable Brethren and Beloved Children, that the Encyclical of Our Predecessor of happy memory had in view chiefly that economic system, wherein, generally, some provide capital while others provide labor for a joint economic activity. And in a happy phrase he described it thus: "Neither capital can do without labor, nor labor without capital."[53] 101. With all his energy Leo XIII sought to adjust this economic system according to the norms of right order; hence, it is evident that this system is not to be condemned **in itself**. And surely it is not of its own nature vicious. **But** it does violate right order when capital hires workers, that is, the non-owning working class, with a view to and under such terms that it directs business and even the whole economic system according to its own will and advantage, scorning the human dignity of the workers, the social character of economic activity and social justice itself, and the common good."

I have already pointed out that Pope Pius XI originally stated that such a syndicate system was voluntary, but later on he states that it is a **duty** to establish it, which change in opinion is understandable as successful producers will be loath to join such a system. It must be forced on them at the point of a gun. Which Pope Pius XI is infallible? And if these are indeed infallible statements, then can not the same be said about Pope Leo XIII, when he definitively declares that such a guild system is a violation of important duties in *LONGINQUA?*

There can only be one conclusion: Pope Pius XI was not exercising the charism of infallibility when he made these statements. They rested on error and incomplete knowledge. At this time the Austrian work demonstrating that the business cycle was caused by guild banking was not widely known. That the horrible Great Depression, of which Pope Pius XI was living through, was caused by inflation and government interference was also poorly understood. It is understandable that Pope Pius XI would come to these conclusions when such studies were in their infancy.

We shall analyze one aspect of his writing to further demonstrate his error: "It happens all too frequently, however, under the salary system, that individual employers are helpless to ensure justice unless, with a view to its practice, they organize institutions the object of which **is to prevent competition** incompatible with fair treatment for the workers."

Note what is going on during a depression (in this case the Great Depression). Previously the erroneous policies of the banking guild have misallocated capital to untenable industries. (We even have an example of this today: consider the construction worker.) And in these industries many workers are hired, who are basically in the business of destroying capital. What then must be done? Clearly these workers must be forced out of this business. To do this, wages must collapse in unsupportable industries. It is to this that Pope Pius XI is referencing when he discusses the "fair treatment of workers.". However this erroneous practice of trying to support the wage level of workers in (rightfully) failing industries is what prolongs the misery. He correctly observed that

51

competition was driving down wages, but he comes to the wrong conclusion. He advocates eliminating competition, which competition is HELPING the economy by eliminating failed industries. His pronouncement therefore rests on an error. For this he can not be faulted.

I will fault him for one thing though. At this time he had an excellent opportunity to renew the Church's condemnation of usury, and to study its application in the modern economy. He barely mentions it in one sentence. That usury contributes to the boom, and the resulting bust, I have already discussed.

Also it must be mentioned that Pope Pius XI was aware of the counter arguments against the syndicate system he was asking to be considered in QA: "We are compelled to say that to Our certain knowledge there are not wanting some who fear that the State, instead of confining itself as it ought to the furnishing of necessary and adequate assistance, is substituting itself for free activity; that the new syndical and corporative order savors too much of an involved and political system of administration; and that (in spite of those more general advantages mentioned above, which are of course fully admitted) it rather serves particular political ends than leads to the reconstruction and promotion of a better social order." Then – silence. He does not comment on these sincere objections.

This then ends my discussion on the claim that Distributism is the "Catholic" system. It is a claim honestly made, but it is erroneous. Next I will analyze the individual elements of the distributist system and why it failed whenever tried.

First is the requirement that the crafts be forcibly organized into guilds. I have discussed this previously under competition and will repeat the conclusions. First the guild will have no idea of what price to charge, i.e., the Calculation Problem. In this system there is no market, so the guild must invent a price. Since they are not omniscient, they will always fail, and misallocations will result. And then we are left to question WHICH price they will set. While we can assume that the plumbers' hourly rate will be set by the guild, we are left with the problem of pricing for pipe and fittings. Will the guild set this, or the pipe and fitting syndicate? Or will the mining syndicate be involved, since they provide the steel? Or how about the PVC syndicate or the oil refinery syndicate? We are left with a warren of unanswered questions. Keep in mind that there is no market. Pesch provided an answer, that an OBJECTIVE determination can be established by consulting everyone's VIEWS. A sane observer will quickly observe that the Government will eventually set the price (how? Who knows.), as this will be a case where they will have to "arbitrate". Hence the term "guild socialism" seems very appropriate.

Second, the guild system rests on the premise that man is not fallen. The guild is given coercive powers and therefore it is NECESSARY to presuppose that they will not abuse those powers. Otherwise we have left society with little protection against corruption. An intelligent reader will observe the shenanigans of Chicago politics and draw his own conclusions about how this will end up.

The next element involves the syndicate system for larger industries, where the company is governed by labor and the owners. Again, the lack of omniscience will become apparent, and Original Sin will show itself in the greed of the various parties. Once again the government will be called in time and time again to arbitrate. And Original Sin dictates that the government will only consider one thing: Who has the most votes?

Finally we have the land redistribution scheme (again to satisfy their obsession with small farming). On this both Pope Leo XIII and Pope Pius XI commented. Here is Pope Pius XI quoting Pope Leo XIII: "Wherefore the wise Pontiff declared that it is grossly unjust for a State to exhaust private wealth through the weight of imposts and taxes."*QA* So much for the property tax extortion scheme of distributists. We also have the defense of private property which was presented in the first section of this book in the Catholic Encyclicals. I won't requote them here.

In closing, I would like the reader to consider three actual guilds operating in the USA. The first two are somewhat limited, but the third is fully functioning, and the errors it has committed bear studying, as the same sorts of errors will be present in any guild.

First we must consider the Doctors' guild called the AMA and the Lawyers' guild called the ABA. In both cases these guilds have used the coercive power of the State to limit competition. For doctors, they have made it illegal for me to use a former military medic to service my medical needs. The result has been that doctors have become very rich, and that there is a shortage of doctors with the resulting high price.

The same is seen with the ABA. Because of their efforts it is illegal for me to use an independent paralegal to prepare a contract for me. The result again is that lawyers have become excessively wealthy.

And finally we will consider the only example I know of for a fully functioning guild in the USA (though closed-shop unionism is another example). That is the Federal Reserve bankers' guild. The Distributist will object, but the fact remains that this can only be labeled a guild:

1. It is private.

2. It is government sponsored.

3. It determines who can enter the trade.

4. It regulates the trade.

5. It determines the "price", in this case the interest rate.

I hope by now, at the end of this section, the reader can independently predict the errors that will be committed by this guild. First is the problem of human fallibility. We are not omniscient. The banking guild will never know the "right" price for money. This was clearly demonstrated in 2004 when the guild set interest rates at 1% and set off the housing boom. This problem will be present in every guild, either with banking, plumbing, or with electricians. Absent a free market, there is no way to determine the price.

Second, man is fallen. When the time came for the Fed guild to raise interest rates (I guess, or rather, their guess), it failed. It was more concerned with Human Respect (a common trait due to Original Sin) than doing the right thing, i.e. making the economy take its medicine by raising rates. The same will be evident in most guilds, there will be temptations for corruption and favoritism. And Man will fail. This is unavoidable when there is a lack of competition.

And thus ends my discussion on the Catholic teachings on economics. In the next two sections I will apply these teachings to our economic problems.

IDEALISM

For this section I will present the economic policies (rather changes) that would be required to save the USA from collapse and establish a sustainable economy. For this we will assume that I am made the dictator of the country, and further, *per impossibile*, that Original Sin would not rise up and cause my corruption.

The section is entitled Idealism, and the reason will soon be self evident. These changes will never happen. I write this section only for those who will survive the collapse, in the hopes that they can establish such a Catholic system. Here then is my program of changes:

1. The USA would be declared a Catholic Confessional State and the Social Kingship of Christ would be proclaimed. Abortion, sodomy, and divorce would be outlawed.

2. A fast involving actual sack cloth would be proclaimed for three days in reparation for the babies we have slaughtered and our sexual sins committed.

3. The USA would be consecrated to the Immaculate Heart of Mary by all of the US bishops.

4. Diplomatic pressure would be put on the Vatican to release the words of Our Lady explaining the Fatima vision, and for the Vatican to consecrate Russia with all of the bishops of the world to Mary's Immaculate Heart.

Note that the previous four steps are probably all that would be required of a dictator, and in fact are absolutely necessary if we are to save this country. However, since this is a book on Catholic Economics, and also because we should never presume on God's mercy, below are the economic changes that would be required:

5. The Federal Reserve Bankers' Guild would be abolished. All guild assets would be transferred to the treasury. Over

time banks would unwind their positions and pay back their liabilities (Treasury assets) until we returned to 100% reserve banking, that is, all loans would be backed by paid-in capital and savings deposits. Fractional reserve lending would be outlawed, and the US dollar would be returned to the gold standard, backed 100% by gold. By this action inflation would be eliminated and the business cycle would cease. Instead investments would only be made out of real saved capital.

6. Usury would be outlawed. Credit cards would be converted to debit cards, and the government would cease making interest payments on public debt. Student loans would continue, as they produce a real return, but the government guarantee would be eliminated, and such loans could be cleared in bankruptcy court. In this way another contributing factor to the business cycle would be eliminated, the great Moral Hazard removed. We would return to a pay-as-you-go society. Furthermore the changes to student loans would eventually cut the cost of a college education in half as professors would be forced to take serious pay cuts as the unending cash pouring in with government guaranteed loans would be eliminated.

7. The previous profits of any bank which required a bail out would be thoroughly reviewed. Any income from "paper" profits resulting from insuring subprime junk loans, whereby the difference between the price of insured junk vs. AAA paper is booked as "profit", would be declared fraudulent, and bonuses awarded on the basis of this fraud would be clawed back.

8. The Community Reinvestment Act (CRA) would be repealed. All government housing agencies such as Fannie Mae and Freddie Mac would be cut off from public support. The bonuses given to Franklin Raines, Jamie

Gorlock, and Rahm Emmanuel would be clawed back.

9. The Tenth Amendment would be strictly enforced. The size of the Federal Government would be reduced to about 10% the current size, or about $300 Billlion, from the $3.2 Trillion of today. $200 Billion would probably be allocated to National Defense.

10. Social Security would be eliminated. Instead the so-called Trust Fund would be distributed pro-rated to anyone who paid into the ponzi scheme in the form of zero coupon bonds. Those already on Social Security who have no other source of income would be paid a monthly stipend out of the General Fund. This would be phased out after about 15 years. In the place of Social Security, all workers would be required to invest 5% of their pay in a private retirement account. This account would be protected from any and all lawsuits and government fines.

11. Medicare would be eliminated. Those already on Medicare would receive an annual lump-sum payment out of the General Fund based on what is available. Keep in mind that further reforms, listed below, would drop the cost of medical care to about 30% the current level, and Catholic Relief Societies would take up the slack due to the huge drop in taxes. After about 15 years Medicare would cease to exist.

12. All income taxes, payroll taxes, and property taxes would be outlawed on the Federal and State/Local levels. The only allowable taxes would be a sales tax, a poll tax (whereby an equal fixed fee is charged to everyone), and an import duty at the Federal level. Parish priests could issue a dispensation for the poll tax for the needy.

13. The current tax system at the Federal level would be

replaced with a flat 10% import duty, and the FAIR tax, which considering the inclusion of the import tariff and the 90% cut in Federal spending, would probably run around 16% in the beginning, and be cut as current retirees depending on Social Security and Medicare pass away

The mechanism of the FAIR tax and its advantages needs to be discussed. The FAIR tax would be a national sales tax on all retail goods and services. Products and services used in production would not be taxed.

Some have raised the concern that the poor would be hit by this tax, so periodically (monthly or annually) a rebate would be sent out to everyone, regardless of income, that covered the tax on a certain minimum of purchases that a poor person would make. This eliminates the concern that this tax would be onerous for the poor. This is how a FAIR tax is differentiated from a national sales tax.

The FAIR tax would be hugely advantageous to production in the USA. Consider a US manufacturer competing against a European firm. The US manufacturer would have zero taxes to pay. Gone would be income taxes, payroll taxes, unemployment taxes, and property taxes. Furthermore, all of the US suppliers to this manufacturer would have this tax advantage. The European manufacturer would have all of these (European) taxes embedded in the price, on top of the 10% import duty. Furthermore, when both the American product and the European product were presented for sale, they would both equally be taxed at 16%.

This advantage also transfers over to US exporters, as all exports would carry zero tax burden. This one change, replacing all taxes with the FAIR tax, would probably solve 80% of the problems in the US economy. The reader is encouraged to research the FAIR tax on the Internet.

14. Most of the Federal regulatory authority would be eliminated, and regulations repealed. Gone would be the EPA, OSHA, EEOC, and NLRB. These function would be transferred to ALREADY EXISTING State agencies. Subsidiarity would rule.

15. The US would withdraw from the fraudulent "Global Warming" agreements. All subsidies for "Green Industries" like solar, bio-fuels, and windfarms would be eliminated. In fact all government subsidies for anything would be outlawed, including agricultural subsidies.

16. Yucca Mountain, the proposed nuclear disposal site, would be opened. The nuclear industry would be deregulated and licensing streamlined. The market would decide whether to keep with a Uranium based industry, or to convert over to Thorium.

17. Foreign aid would be eliminated, including to Israel, and our "allies" would be notified that the US was withdrawing troops from bases outside of US territories over a period of 5 years.

18. Illegal immigration would be thoroughly policed and shutdown. The border would be manned by US troops. All employers would be forced to verify the resident status of all workers with an instantaneous check. The requirements for citizenship would be reformed such that one parent of a US born baby must be at a minimum a green card holder in order for the baby to become a US citizen. Work permits for foreigners would be considered after welfare reforms were enacted depending on labor availability. The permits would be sold annually at the cost of 5% of wages.

19. Government payments for education would be eliminated. At the State level education vouchers, with no strings attached, would be allowed.

20. The labor movement would be reformed. "Nationals" would be outlawed. All unions would be at the local level only. Protection against discrimination would still be in place for locals. Collective bargaining would be limited to wages and work conditions (hours and safety). Work rules could not be discussed, nor sick leave. Locals would be required to maintain a charter that must be certified annually by the Diocesan bishop.

21. Due to the severe conflict of interest, public unions would be outlawed.

22. The Civil Court system would be reformed. Punitive "damages" and treble "damages" would be eliminated as they violate the due process clause. For private disputes, trials would be in front of a panel of three judges. Juries would be eliminated. For lawsuits against the government, trial by jury would be maintained. Caps would be placed on things like "pain-and-suffering" and damages would be limited to actual damages and these "capped" damages.

23. The medical industry would be reformed. Medical licenses would be issued to all applicants. These licenses could be revoked after a trial for malpractice. The only requirement is that medical practitioners would be required to post their credentials in a conspicuous place. With this change a former army medic could practice medicine with the only requirement that his training and background would be posted. His credentials would also mention whether he had received his MD. From my observations, this reform coupled with malpractice reform would lower

medical costs to approximately 30% of current levels.

25. Pharmacists would be allowed to write prescriptions and sell drugs without the involvement of a doctor.

26. Medical malpractice would also be reformed. Damages would be limited to actual damages and certain "capped" damages such as pain-and-suffering.

27. People would be allowed to purchase health insurance across State lines.

28. The same reform in licensing would be implemented for lawyers. Any applicant would be admitted to the bar, and their license could only be revoked after a conviction for malpractice. Again, all legal professionals would be required to post their credentials.

29. Welfare and all other transfer payments would be eliminated. Relief of the poor would be subsumed by Catholic Relief Societies. The Federal Government for only a 5 year period would provide start-up funding for voluntary work co-ops located near industries currently serviced by illegal aliens, such as the food processing industries. Any indigent person, certified as such by a parish priest, could join the co-op. He would be provided with living arrangements and would receive ownership shares in the co-op each year that paid a dividend, in addition to his pay. Over time his ownership interest and dividends would increase. If he left the co-op, or was fired, his ownership would be repurchased by the co-op at a fixed price. Again this would be a strictly voluntary arrangement.

30. Fornication and adultery would be outlawed. The grandparents of any illegitimate babies would be required

to provide money to support the baby.

31. Permits for oil drilling would be streamlined. The US would open up offshore waters and Alaska for oil and gas exploration. Pipeline permits would also be streamlined, and the Keystone Pipeline from Canada would be approved.

32. The Homeland Security Act would be repealed. In its place the government would depend on profiling to protect the country from terrorists. The Moslem religion and country-of-origin would be taken into consideration, and people matching a Moslem terrorist profile would be subject to further security measures. Most passengers on airlines would only be required to go through the metal detector and the baggage x-ray.

32. Immigration would be reformed. Countries with a Catholic populace would take precedence, followed by Protestant countries. Individuals with experience with key technologies would be given preference. Work permits would be strictly curtailed, and thus pressure put on colleges to provide the training that industry needs.

These then are my proposed reforms to the US economic system. They all share the common theme of Subsidiarity, pushing power down to the lowest levels, and the recognition of the Social Reign of Christ the King.

These reforms will never happened, this side of a total collapse. In fact I would be surprised if even one were able to be enacted in our dysfunctional society. My hope is that those who survive to rebuild will take these reforms into consideration.

I say "this side of a total collapse". And a collapse is surely on our doorsteps, a Chastisement from God for the slaughter of millions.

Israel was wiped out over the their murder of perhaps a few thousand babies in the furnaces of Moloch. We have slaughtered millions. Our fate is sealed, the errors of Russia have already spread. All that is left for us is to prepare. Which I discuss in the last section.

REALISM

A IS A

The United States has entered into an economic mess that is now politically impossible to solve. It is Detroit writ large. There are only 3 possible outcomes to this situation. I will only discuss the last one in depth:

1. Fix it. I've shown how in the previous section of the book. Such a plan would result in a severe recession lasting less than 2 years, similar to the Forgotten Depression of 1921. Afterwards we'd have a very healthy boom in growth based on real savings and investments. Unfortunately this is politically impossible and will not happen.

Consider Social Security. Just to balance the payments with taxes seniors would have to immediately take a cut down to 76% of current payments. However that does not fix it. If we want to allow young adults to save 5% of their pay in a private retirement plan, seniors would need a further cut and would only receive 50% of current payments. It gets worse. Social Security will get more and more out of balance as the years go by, so a good estimate is that seniors would have to have their payments cut to 40% of current value. In 20 years Social Security payments would decrease and we could start cutting payroll taxes more until the last Baby Boomer dies. Note that the young adults of today would not receive a penny from their payroll taxes, but at least they would have some savings.

Medicare is so bankrupt there is no way to save it. However busting up the Medical Monopoly would result in a 70% reduction in costs, so it can be fixed. The Medical Monopoly is too strong politically, so this won't happen. Therefore the odds of Option 1 are zero percent.

2. The USA descends into a Third World fever swamp – forever. Unfortunately this is the likely outcome. If you want to see our future, look at Mexico or Venezuela. The Looters and Takers reach 70% of the population and a reform becomes impossible.

As an aside, we should use the terms "Makers/Takers" or "Producers/Looters" instead of the popular "99%/1%".

A billionaire who runs a productive company is a Maker or a Producer. A billionaire banker who makes his money due to the usury and inflation of the bankers' guild is a Taker. Both are the 1%, however one produces and one loots.

Or consider that I, a person who works hard every day, am lumped into the same group as a welfare bum. No, I am a Maker and the bum is a taker.

3. The third option is catastrophic collapse followed by a revolution, or secession, in either case the current system is destroyed (again assuming that we don't descend into a Third World fever swamp forever). To start this more detailed discussion, I'll try my hand as a fiction writer:

Clay could not keep from grinning. This was the first day, and he was standing watch for Alpha base at 5:30 a.m. watching the sky slowly lighten up. It was a crisp day and beautiful. He could not suppress his grin. Finally. Finally the government had gone too far, sliced off one slice too many. They had forgotten patience when they declared that all arms had to be registered.

The Patriots Army had finally made their decision. They declared the Federal Government illegitimate and began the 24/7 occupation of their three bases: Alpha, Beta, and Delta. Clay and his compatriots were pleased by this decision for the citizens would finally fight back against the usurpers of the Constitution. He grinned as he recalled these developments and looked again at the beautiful sunrise. These were the last thoughts he would have on this Earth.

At that moment he was caught by 5 rounds of .308 that cut him in half. Two Kiowa helicopters had come in low, following the valley, and caught him by surprise. Over the next half hour Alpha base was hosed down by machine gun fire. The clean up crew only had to deal with a few survivors.

The scene was more grisly at Beta. The government had decided on using armored personnel carriers to eliminate that target. A young mother and her baby were run down by an APC (the driver had been drinking only a few hours earlier). The Patriots scored better during this engagement, killing one drunken soldier who left his APC, but they were eventually wiped out.

Delta was a complete loss. The government decided to use mortar teams. The defenders never saw it coming, and never fired a shot. And thus ended the revolt by the Patriots Army.

I start with this imaginary story to prove a point. Armed resistance by a private group is futile. You can not overcome the advantage of armor, airpower, mortars, artillery, and now unmanned drones. IF you wanted to mount an armed resistance, an assault rifle would be useless. Instead you would be better served with a subsonic .22, a long range rifle such as a bolt action Savage chambered in perhaps .25-06, and IEDs. I STRONGLY recommend against this, as chances of success are basically zero, with only a few dead men to show for these efforts.

I also want to point out that the army today would not fire on citizens. And I loudly applaud the actions of such organizations as Oath Keepers, whose goal is to make sure it never does. But, we must be prudent, and we must wonder why Oath Keepers is needed in the first place. The army is being degraded, especially with the inclusion of openly homosexual people in its ranks. If the government follows in the footsteps of the Roman Empire, eventually illegal immigrants, perhaps ex-commies, will be added to the ranks. People who have few qualms about following orders to fire on citizens.

It also must be pointed out that already not a few policemen have harassed citizens who have patriot-type messages on bumper stickers. If the police are capable of this, then why not a "properly" indoctrinated army? Perhaps even special units chosen based on a proper "perspective"? Again, I am confident in the current army, but that confidence is waning, especially after the homosexual fiasco. Moral leaders are already leaving. What does that leave behind?

So private armed resistance is basically futile. What then can be done, especially if we want to actively make changes, and not just prepare for the collapse? The answer lies in the problem of "legitimacy". If you read any psy-ops manual, you will discover that the central theme will be about legitimacy. Efforts will be made to make the "good guys" legitimate, and to de-legitimatize the "bad guys". An example will illustrate this concept.

Suppose that you live in a very close-knit community. Perhaps it is a neighborhood with only one road leading in. The neighbors share many common interests, and weekends are marked with open-house parties. The men favor the outdoors and sports, and all are armed.

Now suppose that one neighbor, call him Mike, gets into an altercation with a local gang. The neighborhood finds out that the gang will retaliate by sending three guys in a specific car at a specific time to Mike's house. The thugs will break into Mike's house and execute him, then steal his children and wife, who will be forced to star in porn movies. All to send a message. What would happen when the car with three thugs shows up at Mike's house at the precise time? Will not the thugs be killed in a hail of gunfire?

Now let's change things a bit. Suppose instead that Mike comes to the sane conclusion that the Central Government is illegitimate, especially with regards to the 10th Amendment. So Mike declares

70

that he will pay no more taxes to this criminal organization, which also facilitates the slaughter of babies. Now let us suppose that instead of the thugs car, a car shows up with a special light on top. Instead of thugs, men exit with a special piece of metal pinned to their shirts, and special uniforms. They go in and haul off Mike to be raped for 10 years in prison, along with his wife who spends ten years with Pat the bull dyke, and the kids go into foster care where they star in illegal porn films. Will this be allowed to happen? Of course it will. The neighbors will not fire a shot. And thus you can understand the problem of legitimacy.

For this problem of legitimacy will keep most "good" citizens from joining the cause. Again, armed resistance by a private army is futile. It rarely "catches on". Only overt, extreme acts by the government will cause it to lose legitimacy, and the government knows this. Is there any hope then for the producers to escape the looters, estimated currently at 47% of the population?

Well there is some hope that the Tea Party will gain a majority eventually. The takeover of Wisconsin by the Tea Party was quite a surprise, and they brought an adult budget to that State. A Tea Party majority in Congress would keep taxes low, and reign in spending. So yes there is some hope. But I doubt they can do much with Social Security and Medicare, and there in probably lies our doom. Furthermore, any Tea Party takeover would last at best 2 years, and then they'd be voted out of office once they started cutting the budget.

So if the electoral process is exhausted, what then are we to do? The answer lies in one word: secession. If a group of States seceded from the Union, then the problem of legitimacy is solved. Furthermore the leaders of this new confederacy would have the truth on their side, a huge
advantage. People will only rarely rally around a private army, the failed Occupy Wallstreet is a current example, but they will certainly rally around the leadership of a legitimate State

government.

Is this possible? I believe so. I believe that a secession could occur in the the Plain States and certain Mountain States. In this list I include Texas, Oklahoma, possibly Kansas, Nebraska, the Dakotas, Montana, Idaho, Wyoming, Utah, and Alaska. Perhaps a few Southern States would join, but many have been infested by carpet baggers who have proclaimed a New South.

And we have come close. Few people outside of the Southern Plains realize that a secessionist governor, Randy Brogden, almost got elected in Oklahoma. Only the treachery of Sarah Palin, who in the last few months of the primary came out in support of her "Mama Grizzly" Mary Fallin, stabbing the Tea Party in the back, kept Brogden from winning. It was that close. Furthermore Texas governors have spoken in support of secession, and even passed legislation to start a State bullion bank. So secession is a possibility. What then can the private citizen do to support this movement?

Again, we get back to legitimacy. Every LEGAL effort at de-legitamizing the Federal (Central) government should be undertaken, which is as simple as telling the truth. This includes posting on online forums, Youtube posts, podcasts, and leaking embarrassing stories about government corruption to the press. Stories about Solyndra, bailouts, Benghazi, and Fast-and-Furious have been a gift to those who support the Secessionist cause. More efforts can be made by the private citizen and include providing donations to such causes as Oath Keepers, Pro-Life movements, and the Tea Party.

Beyond secession, the only last thing to consider is surviving the collapse, which I will now address.
To begin, I must make predictions as to what will happen. This is difficult as things are moving quickly, and future events that I predict may already come to past by the time you are reading this.

But I will make an effort.

The common theme is the debt implosion, caused by the Greenspan inflation launched by the guild around 2002. This inflation MASSIVELY misallocated the economy, and coupled with the "ownership society" and the CRA led to a huge increase in unserviceable debt. We are talking about a wipe-out in the Trillions. This could have been solved in 2008 by a large dose of medicine, which medicine included a severe depression. Now, coupled with the strains of the retiring baby boomers, it is too late. The Fed did not fix things, but instead launched QE (whatever version, it is hard to keep track) and launched the biggest financial boom in the history of mankind which is still inflating.

I must also present this from a Catholic perspective. We already have a pretty good guess about what lies in the Fatima secret. The revealed "vision" was telling enough. That the Pope starts out not "ruling" the mountain with the cross, which is a kingdom – the Catholic Church, tells us all we need to know. That the Church will be in serious decline and schism. Furthermore, we can guess at the message after what Pope Pius XII revealed before becoming Pope in 1931, which I will quote: "I am worried by the Blessed Virgin's messages to Lucy of Fatima. This persistence of Mary about the dangers which menace the Church is a divine warning against **the suicide of altering the Faith, in Her liturgy, Her theology** and Her soul…. I hear all around me innovators who wish to dismantle the Sacred Chapel, destroy the universal flame of the Church, reject her ornaments **and make her feel remorse for her historical past.**
A day will come when the civilized world will deny its God, when the Church will doubt as Peter doubted. She will be tempted to believe that man has become God. In our churches, **Christians will search in vain for the red lamp where God awaits them.** Like Mary Magdalene, weeping before the empty tomb, they will ask, "Where have they taken Him?" Note that in none of the revealed messages from Fatima is there any warning about the altering of the Faith or the Mass.

We also have this message revealed by Jesus Himself in 1929 in Tuy: "'Make it known to My ministers, given that they follow the example of the King of

73

France in delaying the execution of My command, **they will follow him into misfortune.** It is never too late to have recourse to Jesus and Mary.'" The King of France fell 100 years to the day after the request to consecrate France to the Sacred Heart of Jesus was ignored. This gives us a hint about timing.

For 100 years after Fatima brings us to 2017, though for the pessimist, it could also be 2029. It is my guess that in 2017 the vision of Fatima will be carried out, i.e. the Pope will be executed by an invading army, perhaps Chinese (the Red Dragon), Russian, or Moslem. If nothing happens in 2017, then 2029 comes into play. That would mean 12 more years of even worse moral and economic conditions. I dread the thought.

I also firmly believe, based on the message written on the revealed envelope, that the Consecration of Russia was required sometime in the early 60s, soon after the message was supposed to be revealed in 1960. And this has yet to occur. And here is where it gets very serious. One of the errors of Russia was abortion. And it has proceeded throughout our society such that we have slaughtered tens of millions of babies. For the offense of slaughtering perhaps "mere" thousands of infants in the furnaces of Moloch, Israel was destroyed. We have killed tens of millions. This would have been prevented it the consecration had been carried out in the early 60s (it still remains to be done). I conclude that it is too late. The errors of Russia HAVE spread, millions of babies HAVE been slaughtered by our own hands; this is now in the past (though the slaughter continues). And we must pay the price. If you wish to do more research into the Errors of Russia, search "Yuri Bezmenov Demoralization" on Youtube, which has a collection of talks given by this KGB defector.

And so we are left to ponder what we must do to prepare. First and foremost is to get right with God. Flee to the confessional. And say daily your family Rosary. For those who doubt that the Secret (at least the interpretation of the vision) is still hidden, consider this quote from the Vatican in 1960: "... it is most likely that the letter will never be opened, in which Sister Lucy wrote down the words which Our Lady confided as a secret to the three shepherds of the Cova da Iria." In what has been revealed so far, there are no words from our Lady. The letter has not been revealed, only the vision which was contained in a notebook. More from Sr. Lucy, written long before this controversy arose: "I have written what you asked me; God willed to try me a little, but finally this was indeed His will: (the text) is sealed in an envelope and it is in the notebooks ..." and the following: "'You have already made known two parts of the Secret. When will the time arrive for the third part?' 'I communicated the third part *in a letter* to the Bishop of Leiria,' she answered. All that was revealed was a notebook, no letter was produced. Our Lady's words have yet to be revealed. This I have proved.

So we know that the Chastisement, punishment for the slaughter of the innocents, is upon us. Beyond religious preparations, we must consider our temporal affairs. But before I do, I must stress that we all must face death. Does it really matter in the end if it is due to a heart attack or from being gunned down by an angry hoard of gang-bangers? Get right with God.

We return again to timing. There appears to be a race as to who will collapse first. Italy, Greece, Spain, China, or Japan all seem like likely candidates to set it off. A war with Russia is not improbable or perhaps a major terrorist event. One thing is for certain, the debts we have can not be paid back. It is impossible.

When the debt collapse occurs, taking into consideration Original Sin, I predict that there will be additional massive money printing by the Fed, ECB, and Bank of Japan, which money will be used to buy up government debt. This will buy a little time (if any due to the loss of confidence), perhaps weeks, perhaps months. The results of this inflation will be devaluation and rising prices. Von Mises labeled this the "Crack-up Boom", and the reason he gave it this title is self-evident. At this point we will resemble Venezuela.

What follows will be the Greater Depression on steroids. Misery and hunger will be widespread. To prepare, the single best thing you can do is to relocate your family to a small town in a rural area where people know each other. However this is only an option if you can secure employment, which is not easy. I can not stress enough the importance of moving away from large urban areas if at all possible. These places will see bankruptcy, hunger -- possibly even starvation, riots, and crime. Just imagine what the ghetto areas in your nearby city will look like when the checks get cut off. This will happen after a collapse.

For those who can not make the move, you are reduced to basic survival. This includes acquiring freeze dried food, bleach for water, guns, cash, and junk silver coins. Details about this go beyond the scope of a book on Catholic Economics, so instead of commenting further I suggest that the reader research the topic of urban survival on the Internet.

After the world wide collapse, it is inevitable that war will break out. For this we must strongly suspect that the Red Dragon of China will be unleashed until it stands upon the sands of the Mediterranean Sea. What this will involve, I can not hope to predict at this time.

These then are my predictions, a final collapse and another World War. There is some hope with the Tea Party, and still more with secession. But I am a realist and do not have much Faith in fallen man. Politicians will not enact the reforms needed until it is forced upon them. Witness the fiascoes of Greece and Detroit. Men everywhere share this Fallen Nature. Prepare accordingly.

Appendix

A. Americanism

Rampant in the writings of the Distributists and Monarchists on the various Traditional Catholic internet forums and also in their books is the BIG LIE of the heresy called "Americanism". This heresy is usually defined as supporting a republican form of government, free market capitalism, and the Constitution. It is a big lie.

There actually WAS an heresy called "Americanism", however it has nothing to do with the above. The Americanism Heresy was prevalent IN EUROPE. Europeans in CATHOLIC CONFESSIONAL STATES declared that since the Catholic Church was successful in America, there was no need in Europe to have a Catholic Confessional State. The heresy was particularly strong in France.

Pope Leo XII commented on this heresy:

> 6. The main factor, no doubt, in bringing things into this happy state were the ordinances and decrees of your synods, especially of those which in more recent times were convened and confirmed by the authority of the Apostolic See. But, moreover (a fact which it gives pleasure to acknowledge), thanks are due to the equity of the laws which obtain in America and to the customs of the well-ordered Republic. For the Church amongst you, unopposed by the Constitution and government of your nation, fettered by no hostile legislation, protected against violence by the common laws and the impartiality of the tribunals, is free to live and act without hindrance. Yet, though all this is true, **it would be very erroneous to draw the conclusion that in America is to be sought the type of the most desirable status of the Church**, or that it would be **universally** lawful or expedient for State and Church to be, as in America, dissevered and divorced. The fact that Catholicity with you is in good condition, nay, is even enjoying a prosperous growth, is by all means to be attributed to the fecundity with which God has endowed His Church, in virtue of which unless men or circumstances interfere, she spontaneously expands and propagates herself; but she would bring forth **more** abundant fruits **if, in addition to liberty, she enjoyed the favor of the laws and the patronage of the public authority.**"

Pope Leo XIII goes on to condemn certain beliefs of the Americanism Heresy: absolute freedom of the press, absolute religious freedom, and separation of Church and State. Note that this is only pertinent for Catholic Confessional States. This is easily proven as the last thing American Catholics want is a

State Protestant Religion imposed on them.

As an aside, Pope Leo XIII in one of his encyclicals on "Americanism" appears to prophesize about the horror which is known as Vatican II:

"The underlying principle of these new opinions is that, in order to more easily attract those who differ from her, the Church should shape her teachings more in accord with the spirit of the age and relax some of her ancient severity and make some concessions to new opinions. Many think that these concessions should be made not only in regard to ways of living, but even in regard to doctrines which belong to the deposit of the faith. They contend that it would be opportune, in order to gain those who differ from us, to omit certain points of her teaching which are of lesser importance, and to tone down the meaning which the Church has always attached to them. It does not need many words, beloved son, to prove the falsity of these ideas if the nature and origin of the doctrine which the Church proposes are recalled to mind."

As a quick aside, we must analyze the Monarchists' views. Note that in 99% of the case, when a Catholic says he supports Monarchy, he is supporting an ABSOLUTE Monarchy. So if sonny-boy, the Crown Prince busies himself with snorting coke and chasing whores, the society will have no defense when his father dies. The Monarchist merely presumes on the Mercy of God that He will intervene to save the realm. How this squares away with King Henry VIII, Defender of the Faith, the Sun King, and Czar Nicholas II, they can not explain.

Some Monarchists will lie and say that you espouse the Americanist Heresy if you oppose an ABSOLUTE Monarcy. The reader should consult the quotes from Papal Encyclicals listed at the beginning of this book on the forms of government. Also, he should consider this quote from Pope Leo XIII from the encyclical discussing "Americanism": "Precisely at the epoch when the American colonies, having, **with Catholic aid**, achieved liberty and independence, coalesced into a constitutional Republic the ecclesiastical hierarchy was happily established amongst you; and at the very time when the popular suffrage placed the **great Washington** at the helm of the Republic, the first bishop was set by apostolic authority over the American Church. The well-known friendship and familiar intercourse which subsisted between these two men seems to be an evidence that the United States ought to be conjoined in concord and amity with the Catholic Church."
Readers are encouraged to read the Encyclicals themselves:

http://www.vatican.va/holy_father/leo_xiii/encyclicals/documents/hf_l-xiii_enc_06011895_longinqua_en.html

http://www.papalencyclicals.net/Leo13/l13teste.htm

B. Obamacare

The current (pre-Obamacare) health care system is a catastrophe. The main points for this system are as follows:

1. Most people join their employer's plan and only pay about 20% of the cost of said health plan due to tax policies of the Central Government.
2. The plans are not insurance. They are health plans, which plans cover items dictated by the States. Real Health Insurance is illegal.
3. People are forced to use only doctors who are approved by the AMA Doctor's guild scheme.
4. People must purchase plans only from State approved companies. It is illegal to use out-of-State plans.
5. People must obtain a doctor's prescription if they need medication.
6. Malpractice lawsuits have morphed into a lottery system. They are no longer used to settle legitimate disputes.
7. The costs for obtaining care are high.
8. Hospitals are required to treat everyone in their Emergency Room for free.
9. Due to CON laws and "hospital privleges" moral doctors who choose to operate outside of the system are severely disadvantaged.
10. Medicare, especially the CMS, rewards hospitals for overcharging cash customers and giving discounts to insurance customers by giving them higher reimbursement rates.

Now all of these problems are never looked at in detail, instead we are told that the cost of health "insurance" is too high. This is an error. Given the above conditions, the cost of health plans is reasonable. The problem is that MEDICAL costs are too high due to government protected monopoly schemes. 50 years ago, certainly before Medicare, the doctor CAME TO YOUR HOUSE in what was called a "house call", though he didn't drive a Porsche, nor maintain a ski lodge in Aspen.

Now we consider "Obamacare". Obamacare requires healthy people to purchase these expensive health plans. It also provides a fall-back socialist plan available to everyone. None of the problems listed above are dealt with. When implemented, the unlimited demand unleashed by "free" care, or paid for by plans you are forced to purchase (you might as well get your money's worth) drove up the costs further. As a result, eventually private plans will be canceled until a critical mass of people end up on the socialist plan. This is intentional.

For Obamacare is a poorly disguised attempt to bail out Medicare. By forcing 20 million healthy people into the system, a huge pool of money is made available to fund the medical costs of retirees, a process known as "cost shifting", facilitated by the CMS. When the system collapses, a universal socialist policy will be initiated. Or, the present Obamacare will be kept with no private plans. Note that employers are forced to pay a "penalty" if they don't provide "insurance". This money will be used to fund the medical care of retirees.

Note that no government rationing is needed. As more and more people demand "their" free care, the waiting time for seeing a doctor will naturally increase. This is present today in the Canadian system, which system is nearing bankruptcy. If you use GAAP accounting, the Canadian System IS bankrupt.

In order to solve our medical care crisis, we have to return to a complete free market, and allow the Church to provide medical care for the indigent through Diocesan supported Catholic hospitals, and Catholic Relief Societies. We also need to eliminate illegal immigration.

Specifics on the steps needed to lower medical costs (informally estimated by me to 30% current costs) are listed under the "Idealism" section of this book.

C.   Caritas in Veritate

Below is my analysis of the Encyclical *Caritas in Veritate*, an Encyclical which appears to be authored by several individuals. Fortunately, it is not binding, as the Encyclical so states: "The Church does not have technical solutions to offer[10] and does not claim "to interfere in any way in the politics of States." I will accept this for Caritas in Vertitate, however this is erroneous. The Church clearly offered solutions, it was called *Rerum Novarum*.

The analysis is presented by actual quotations from *Caritas in Veritate*, with my comments afterward. Emphasis in the original is indicated by the use of italics. Sections I have emphasized are indicated in bold. The sections are not in order:

"It (Charity) strives to build the *earthly city* according to law and justice. On the other hand, charity transcends justice and completes it in the logic of giving and forgiving[3]. The *earthly city* is promoted not merely by relationships of rights and duties, but to an even greater and more fundamental extent by relationships of gratuitousness, mercy and communion. (Emphasis in the original)

Now let us rephrase this section with the Traditional Church teaching on the earthly city: "It (Charity) strives to build the *City of the Devil* according to law and justice. On the other hand, charity transcends justice and completes it in the logic of giving and forgiving[3]. The *City of the Devil* is promoted not merely by relationships of rights and duties, but to an even greater and more fundamental extent by relationships of gratuitousness, mercy and communion."

Now you may say that the "earthly city" was a poor choice for Pope Benedict to use. He is not referencing (and opposing) St. Augustine in this section. However, the evidence is conclusive. He most certainly is referencing St. Augustine as can be seen by this further quote from *Caritas in Veritate*:

"Man's earthly activity, when inspired and sustained by charity, contributes to the building of the universal **city of God**, which is the goal of the history of the human family. In an increasingly globalized society, the common good and the effort to obtain it cannot fail to assume the dimensions of the whole human family, that is to say, the community of peoples and nations[5], in such a way as to shape the *earthly city (City of the Devil)* in unity and peace, rendering it to some degree an anticipation and a prefiguration of the undivided **city of God**."

- - -

"It is the primordial truth of God's love, grace bestowed upon us, that opens our

82

lives to gift and makes it possible to hope for a "development of the whole man and of all men"[8], to hope for progress "from less human conditions to those which are **more human**"[9], obtained by overcoming the difficulties that are inevitably encountered along the way." Do we really want to become "more human", a race of FALLEN men?

- - -

"What is meant by the word "decent" in regard to work? It means work that expresses the essential dignity of every man and woman in the context of their particular society: .....work that makes it possible for **families** to meet their needs and provide schooling for their children, without the **children** themselves being forced into labour;" With this statement, the Pope has effectively cut the Living Wage in half, as the Traditional Church teaching is that employers should pay a living wage to a **man**, so that **he** can support his family. Now we are told a company can pay half that wage, but to the family, i.e. both the husband and wife, so that they can support the family. I assume it is a little more than half when you factor in the costs of her "career wear", warehousing the children in stranger-care, and the costs of Ritalin.

- - -

"Today, as we take to heart the lessons of the current economic crisis, which sees the State's *public authorities* directly involved in **correcting** errors and malfunctions, it seems more realistic to *re-evaluate their role* and their powers, which need to be prudently reviewed and remodelled so as to enable them, perhaps through new forms of engagement, to address the challenges of today's world." See Appendix E which analyzes what caused the Greater Depression. Hopefully you already know after reading this book.

- - -

"Here budgetary policies, with cuts in social spending often made under pressure from international financial institutions, can leave citizens **powerless** in the face of old and new risks;" Note the assumption that government must relieve the poor. Go back and read what Pope Leo XIII said about alms giving, located at the beginning of this book.

- - -

"*Economic life* undoubtedly requires *contracts*, in order to regulate relations of exchange between goods of equivalent value. But it also needs *just laws* and *forms of redistribution* governed by politics," Go back and read what Pope Leo XIII said about redistribution of wealth at the beginning of this book. Keep in mind, however, that Pope Benedict XVI clearly states that there are no solutions offered in *Caritas in Vertitate*. I'll take him at his word.

- - -

"In this way he was applying on a global scale the insights and aspirations contained in *Rerum Novarum*, written when, as a result of the Industrial Revolution, **the idea was first proposed** — somewhat ahead of its time — that the civil order, for its self-regulation, also needed intervention from the State **for purposes of redistribution.**" There is no citation because Pope Leo XIII OPPOSED redistribution in Rerum Novarum. This is either a lie, or a grave error. Let's be serious, it's an intentional lie to deceive the public.

- - -

"The different aspects of the crisis, its solutions, and any new development that the future may bring, are increasingly interconnected, they imply one another, they require new efforts of holistic understanding and a *new humanistic synthesis.*" No comment. Emphasis in the original.

- - -

"Because it is a gift **received by everyone**, charity in truth is a force that builds community, it brings all people together without imposing barriers or limits." Charity is a Theological Virtue received by Faith and Baptism. Pagans, moslems, hindus, jews, and animists do not receive this.

- - -

"*The development of peoples depends, **above all**, on a recognition that the human race is a single family* working together in true communion, not simply a group of subjects who happen to live side by side" The development of peoples depends above all on the waters of Baptism and Faith in Jesus Christ, without which Faith it is impossible to be saved.

- - -

Steel yourself with what you are about to read. Keep in mind that the Pope indicated this is not binding:

"67. In the face of the unrelenting growth of global interdependence, there is a strongly felt need, even in the midst of a global recession, for a reform of the *United Nations Organization*, and likewise of *economic institutions and international finance*, so that the concept of the family of nations can acquire **real teeth.** ... *To manage the global economy; to revive economies hit by the* *crisis; to avoid any deterioration of the present crisis and the greater imbalances that would result; to bring about integral and timely disarmament, food security and peace; to guarantee the protection of the environment and to regulate migration: for all this, there is urgent need of a true **world political authority**,* ... *(*a few bones thrown to the dogs about a moral government, which is impossible since the vast majority will not be Catholic in this system, is omitted.) *Furthermore, such an authority would need to be universally recognized and to be vested with the effective **power** to ensure security for all, regard for justice, and respect for rights[148]. Obviously it would have to have the **authority to ensure compliance** with its decisions from all parties, and also with the coordinated measures adopted in various international forums.* " There is no other way to describe this. The Pope is calling for the seating of anti-Christ. I do not ascribe this to sinister intentions, but to a lack of understanding on how the economy works. Also, from the tone of this section, I do not believe these are the words of Pope Benedict XVI, survivor of Nazism. I also strongly suspect that the New World Order has some pretty gruesome photos of homosexual bishops molesting boys.

- - -

"I too wish to recall here the importance of the Second Vatican Council for Paul VI's Encyclical and for the whole of the subsequent social Magisterium of the Popes." No argument from me. To come to these conclusion, you must first start with the Modernist overemphasis on the "Dignity" of Man.

I'll end with a quote from Pope St. Piux X: "What truly is the point of departure of the enemies of religion for the sewing of the great serious errors by which the faith of so many is shaken? They begin by denying that man has fallen by sin and been cast down from his former position. Hence they regard as mere fables original sin and the evils that were its consequence. Humanity vitiated in its source **vitiated in its turn the whole race of man**; and thus was evil introduced amongst men and the necessity for a Redeemer involved. All this rejected, it is easy to understand that no place is left for Christ, for the Church, for grace or for anything that is **above and beyond human nature**; in one word the whole edifice of faith is shaken from top to bottom." (Pius X, Ad Diem Illium Laetissimum, Feb 2, 1904)"

E. Causes of the Greater Depression

There is a rampant accusation by leftists that the Greater Depression is evidence that Capitalism fails; that the greed of capitalists has led us to this inevitable collapse. Nothing could be further from the truth.

Consider, for example, what President George Bush stated during the height of the collapse: "In order to save capitalism, I had to abandon it." This is preposterous, and the error becomes evident when I restate his words as follows: "In order to save usurious banking and the "ownership society", I had to abandon capitalism." Because left to its own practices, the free market would have bankrupted the usurers and eliminated the GOVERNMENT organs of the sub-prime ownership society. So let us analyze what really happened.

First, and absolutely NECESSARY for the collapse was the existence of the banking guild known as the Federal Reserve. Let us consider one aspect of the collapse: the extreme leverage of the usurious bankers (known to leftists as "capitalists"). Isn't this proof of their greed? Yes, of course it is. Now ask yourself: "Where did the money come from to lever up 30:1 (e.g. a bank with $1 Billion in deposits could make "investments" of $30 Billion)?" Can you lever up without money? The money was "printed" by the banking guild and given to the banks to (mal)invest. Doesn't greed, this flaw spawning from Original Sin, argue for the elimination of a banking guild run by a few Fallen men and women? Leaders of a guild are not exempt from The Fall. In actuality the power of that position, coupled with the clouded intellect of man, provides more temptations and more opportunities for catastrophic errors, than a free market system which is highly distributed, and thus tends to oppose Original sin (via competition) and limit the damage caused by errors. This is all that is needed to be known about the Greater Depression. It was caused by the Federal Reserve banking guild pumping too much money. Without this "free" money, leveraging was impossible on this scale. In a 100% reserve, gold-backed system this kind of leverage becomes metaphysically impossible.

Second, we will look at other causes. The epicenter for the crisis, after the guild, was a piece of legislation called the Community Reinvestment Act, which in short requires banks to supply minority quota loans, which loans are called "sub-prime". The banks, however, were caught between a rock and a hard place, especially after "community" agitators started launching lawsuits against them for not complying with the CRA. On one hand, the CRA required them to make these sub-prime loans. On the other hand, the banking guild and the FDIC have strict requirements for the bank's balance sheet. Out of this conflict, the Grand Scheme (my term) was launched.

The banks went ahead with the sub-prime loans. However, Fannie-Mae, run by such leftists as Franklin Raines and Jamie Gorlock, agreed to buy up the loans. Furthermore, Countrywide Financial was given the task of facilitating this business. Countrywide, headed by Angelo Mozilo, and on whose board former Clinton HUD secretary Henry Cisneros sat, established a mortgage packaging brokerage, whereby it bought up sub-prime debt, securitized (bundled) it into Morgage Backed Securities, then sold the MBS to Fannie-Mae. ONE TRILLION dollars of this toxic waste was sold to Fannie, with encouragement sent by Fannie's Franklin Raines to do more. The banks were happy, collecting origination fees, Mozilo was happy with a small mark up due to the volume, and the politicians were happy because they were backing the "ownership society". Mozilo is a free man today, and I imagine he has a lot of emails and taped phone calls in his possession.

Another boogey-man of the leftist is the Credit Default Swap. Pay attention to the last word, SWAP. Chances are high that you have entered into one of these already, though in retail it is called PMI, or Private Mortgage Insurance. Under PMI, if you default, the bank is paid the remaining principle on the house, and the insurance company takes over the mortgage. It can then foreclose, sell the house, and recover some or all of its losses.

CDS's work the same way. The writer or issuer agrees to pay out the notional value of the insured debt in exchange for receiving ownership of the debt instrument and a fee. We will concern ourselves with CDS's issued on MBS.

There is nothing wrong or immoral with CDS's. In an economy absent a banker's guild, home prices would stay relatively constant, or perhaps appreciate say 1% per year. During the Great Banker's Guild boom of the "aughts", houses would increase at 10% per year. This was artificial, with the machinations of the guild causing the markets to LIE.

An insurance company that was writing CDS's on bundled mortgages (MBS), would have to go by the market information to price this insurance. So in a 10% rising market, they could make very conservative assumptions, say a 1% annual rise. Think about it, what assumptions would you be forced to make in this situation? They would also assume a standard distribution for failure. Therefore, when a few MBS's defaulted, they would assume they could recover 100% of the notional value on the CDS by foreclosing on the defaulted mortgages and quickly selling the homes into a "hot" market. Furthermore they would have to assume that most of the mortgages packaged in the MBS would be solvent and continue to have value. This is why CDS's were extremely cheap during the boom.

But what did happen? Finally realizing that they had set off a boom, the banking guild decided to raise interest rates due to fears of inflation (and the political repercussions). The outcome of raising rates was the crash of 2008/2009, where some homes lost 50% of their value. The insurance companies that had written CDS's on MBS's were now bankrupt. The loss in home value was huge, and the number of MBS's defaulting far surpassed even the most conservative projections. Furthermore many MBS's saw 70% of their packaged mortgages default. All of this happened at the same time.

We will consider one particular insurance company: AIG. AIG wrote a lot of CDS's. However, this was with their financial arm. Accruals for their insurance arm were strictly segregated and protected by law (this was before Obama and MF Global). Now during this time, Goldman Sachs became convinced that the Greater Depression was inevitable. So in order to hedge against a drop in their investment portfolio, they decided that a very cheap hedge to put on was to buy CDS's, which were indeed very cheaply priced in the era of annual home appreciations of 10%. However, GS did not own any MBS's, a condition described as being "nake short" mortgages. Remember I told you to pay attention to the word swap. The only way they could collect a payoff from their credit default swaps was if they sold the CDS's into the market.

Eventually, after the guild swung interest rates the other way, and destroyed the housing market, the economy came crashing down. AIG was now bankrupt. In a free market it would have been taken over by a court appointed bankruptcy trustee. The insurance arm would emerge the following day, whole, perhaps called New AIG. Policy holders would not be harmed. The financial arm would become say AIG Finance and liquidated by the trustee. He would obtain the MBS's on the other side of the swaps, and foreclose on the houses. Money raised by the sales, added to any reserves AIG had would then be paid to the holders of CDS. Perhaps they would get 75 cents on the dollar, pick a number. Not a catastrophe. Except that GS didn't own the MBS's covered by their CDS's. So it could not collect a penny, and its hedge would have been worthless.

GS suffered heavy losses during the collapse in its other investments and in all probability would have been bankrupt after the collapse. So the other arm of GS, known as the Federal Government, stepped in and took over AIG, preventing the bankruptcy. It paid out 100% on the CDS's, including to GS, which pocketed $13 Billion.

Now ask yourself after reading the previous: Did capitalism fail?

Interested readers are encouraged to obtain two books for an in-depth analysis of the events leading to the Greater Depression: *Architects of Ruin*, by Peter Schwiezer, and *Meltdown* by Thomas Woods.

F. The Labor Theory of Value

I will not spend too much time explaining The Labor Theory of Value in detail as there is a free book online, a masterpiece, titled *Karl Marx and the Close of His System* by Eugen von Bohm-Bawerk, an Austrian economist.

It must be stressed that the Labor Theory of Value is the fundamental premise of the Marxist system, and it is completely erroneous. Marxism simply does not exist apart from it. The Labor Theory states that ALL value in a produced good (or service) comes from the labor inputs. That is, all value should be equivalent to manhours employed in the production of a good.

There are various problems with this theory which are rather obvious:

1. Manhours do not determine value. A Craftsman can make a ring stone out of coal, which takes him weeks to carefully cut, and he could not sell the ring. In a word the value would be next to zero.

2. The theory has a very fundamental flaw: Labor is a COST of production. It does not determine the value of the production; this cost is only used to determine if it is feasible to produce the product GIVEN the value of the produced good. Other COSTS such as machinery, organizational know-how, organizational systems, patents, insurance, legal costs, entrepreneurship (reading the market), and interest are not even considered.

3. The Labor Theory fails at explaining phenomena such as the Tulip Bubble or the price of art.

4. The Labor Theory can not differentiate the difference in value of a clerk vs. a craftsman.

In closing, the Value of a product or service is determined by the subjective opinion of consumers. We call this "demand". Even intermediate goods such as tools and machinery are valued by the prices commanded by the finished goods they will eventually produce. If it takes too many manhours to produce a good for the price determined by consumers, that good will not be produced. We see here again the allocative function of pricing in a Market Economy.

Made in the USA
Coppell, TX
07 March 2021